MW01008079

Does God Really Exist?

It was one of the most startling covers ever published by TIME magazine. On April 6, 1966, they dared to ask a question that many people in ivory towers had already been posing: "Is God dead?" Someone was heard to respond, "I didn't even know He was sick" . . . but there's nothing humorous about the hurt in someone's heart which makes them pose that lonely, eternal question: "Is Anybody out there?"

In this modern age, is there any proof that God exists, or is He just a fairy tale dreamed up to make us feel better about the brutality of our human existence? Are Christians and believers simply inhaling what Karl Marx called the opiate of the masses?

SHAWN: Not too long ago, I was flying across the United States, and I discovered to my delight that my seatmate was a great travel companion. We shared a lot of common interests, so we were able to pass the time quite well. But then the subject of religion came up.

"What do you do for a living?" she asked me.

"Well," I said, "I'm a minister."

A lot of times, that is a conversation-ender, especially on airplanes and on golf courses or at NHL hockey games. But this lady didn't bat an eye. "Wow, that's really interesting, because I'm an atheist."

"Really?" I wasn't sure what else to say, because, to be honest, I don't actually believe in atheists—not if you define "atheist" as someone who knows *for a certainty* there is no God.

She started to explain her lack of faith to me. "Listen, when I was a kid, some pretty awful things happened to me. And when I went to the minister looking for answers, he didn't have any. So even though I still find religion very interesting, I personally don't have much faith that God exists."

So as it turns out, my new friend wasn't really certain that God didn't exist. She was just disappointed with her experience.

This question of God's existence is one that has captivated philosophers and thinkers for hundreds of years. Since neither side of the debate can produce God— or *no God*—in their laboratory test tubes, it comes down to being a matter of faith, whichever way you choose to believe. It is a leap for the Christian and the atheist both. But what evidence can the believer point to in support of his or her choice?

MARK: A number of years ago, I was traveling and preaching in Eastern Europe. I had been very active in Christian ministry there in the late 1980s, when communism still held sway in those countries. When that unforgettable evening in 1989 occurred and the Berlin Wall finally came tumbling down, I was sharing God's Word in Budapest, the capital city of Hungary. It was remarkable to see those thousands of people marching in the streets, celebrating their newfound freedom.

But we also saw an incredible hunger for God, for spiritual things, for Bible reading and moral values. All of those things had been lost for decades behind the Iron Curtain. I was privileged to be right there as universities began to open up their doors to new philosophies. A number of leading institutions invited me to come and speak to their students on the subject of God and the arguments for His existence. These were some fascinating excursions for me!

The president of one of Hungary's top universities came to me directly and asked: "Now, Dr. Finley, would you be willing to come and lecture at our university? We'd like to hear you share with us about the subject of astronomy."

For a moment I was nonplussed. Astronomy–not theology? But he explained that they wanted me to show them—from astronomy—that God existed. And even though I wasn't an astronomer, I did have a lecture prepared, a presentation with some graphic slides on my computer. So I agreed to come.

Then the president said: "Uh, there's just one caveat."

"What's that?"

He explained. "We will also include a professor from our astronomy department. You will speak on why God exists, and then he will speak on why God doesn't exist."

I pondered this for a moment. Frankly, it smelled like a setup. These men wanted to knock a few bricks out of my own "Berlin Wall!" But I quickly replied, saying: "Okay, I'm willing to do that, but now here's *my* condition. Since I am your guest at the university, let your astronomer speak first, then I'll go second, and respond to whatever he says."

To my relief, he agreed. I got to the university at the appointed time and the president met me at the front door. "We have a problem," he confessed. I was afraid he was going to cancel the lecture, but he explained. "Our astronomy professor has another appointment; he is not able to make it."

"No problem at all," I responded. "Let me have the entire two hours with your students. I'll give them my lecture, then we'll open up the floor and they can ask me any questions they want."

So that's what we did. I discussed with them the incredible vastness of space, the glories of the heavens, and the evidence that God exists from *design*. Where there is design, there must be a Designer, I insisted. Where there is creation, there surely must have been a Creator. And so we went over that evidence.

I noticed as we were discussing and fielding questions that the hall had one section where just professors and teachers were sitting. One student appeared to be gesturing and getting some wordless signals from one of the experts sitting among the professors. Apparently some were still hoping to tie this American preacher up in philosophical knots.

Finally the student stood up and posed his question. "Our famous, renowned Soviet astronaut, Ghermon Titov, traveled into space. He was the first one into the heavens. Did he see God up there? No. Have you ever *seen* God? No." And he sat down with a flourish and a buzz of approval from his fellow students.

Just as he was speaking, I felt a flash of inspiration. There are times in a Christian's life when the God you believe in gives a heaven-sent idea. And I knew it! I also knew what this faculty was trying to do. So I said to the young questioner: "You know, before I answer that question, I have a question myself that I want to ask your faculty. Then I'll respond to more student questions."

He nodded his agreement and I began. "Faculty," I said, "let's leave God out of the question. Let's leave the Bible out. I'm a believer. You know that. You folks are not believers. But let's leave all of that out. I just want to ask you one philosophical question. Of all the knowledge in the world, how much do your students have? Do they know 50% of all there is to know? Do they know 80% of all there is to know? How much do they know?"

Now, these were bright young people, and they were

enrolled at one of Hungary's top-flight universities. But I admit that I began to needle them just a little bit. "Let's take the 16th century Ming Dynasty of China. Could any of you give me, in order, the seventeen emperors in that dynasty?" They sat there, wordless. "Or how about Saudi Arabia? Seventh century A.D. Maybe one of you could stand and list for us the first 15 caliphs of that era–along with their wives."

Still there was no response. For some reason, these good-hearted college young people, who knew so much, had discovered a gap in their education.

I continued. "Of the 1,500 known languages in the world today, how many do you speak? Does anyone speak 1,300 of them? If you had to take a test given by the leading astrophysicist in the world, how much would you know? Can you recite for me now the chemical compounds in order? Of all the knowledge that is printed in all of the world's books printed in just this one year, how many have you read?"

The students saw where I was going. I then turned my attention to their teachers. " Professors, as you grade these students, and from an intellectual standpoint, do they know 50% of all there is to know?" They shook their heads. "Do they know 30% of all that there is to know?" No. "How about 20%?" No. I leaned forward a little bit. "I'm going to give your students the benefit of the doubt and say that, as this is such a prestigious university, your students and you surely know 5% of all that there is to know. Even then that means you *don't* know 95% of all that there is to know."

They nodded a reluctant assent to my statement, and I explained what I felt it all meant. "Now, if by your own admission, you only know 5% of all that there is to know, and you *don't* know 95% of what there is to know, how can you possibly be sure that God isn't over in the 95% of knowledge that you don't possess?" It was amazing!

They were all nodding their agreement. They knew, intellectually, that this was a reasonable argument.

Then I gently asserted: "My good friends, if you acknowledge that, then you are not atheists. Because an atheist says, 'I know for absolutely certain that God doesn't exist.' But what you are saying to me today is that He *may* exist. He may exist in the knowledge that you don't have."

But I wasn't finished with these dear people. "I have another question for you," I said. "Let's suppose that in life, there are only these two alternatives. First: there is no God. You and I are all here by evolutionary chance. There is no lasting purpose to life, and you are simply an advanced animal. You live–then you die. You go into the grave. There's nothing after that. Worms eat your body, your bones bleach– and that's it. So, that's one choice. You struggle through life; you claw your way through. You battle through these hard years. Some good things happen to you, some bad. But that is it."

From my years traveling in communist societies, I knew firsthand that I had just described, with quite some accuracy, the life experience of many of these people. And they knew that I knew.

I continued: "On the other hand, there is another alternative. Perhaps there *is* a Creator God who made you. He fashioned you. He shaped you. He loves you. He cares for you in life. And this Creator God who fashioned and shaped you, who loves you so much, also has a plan for your life. He is here with you today. He is present in all that you experience. He desires to give you a full, abundant, blessed life. He wants to help you discover all of the happiness and joy that He intends for you. He wants to expand your mind as you work in this wonderful university. He wants to enable you to be more productive and successful in everything you put your hand to. What's more, He has a marvelous plan that will give you the opportunity to live with Him through all eternity. In this alternative, you can be with this wonderful God forever on the other side of death and the grave. These are the two choices. These are the alternatives every one of us has."

There was a moment of silence in that hall. I had just given them what we sometimes call Pascal's Wager, named for the great French philosopher. He pointed out that if God didn't exist, those who had spent a lifetime "believing" in Him truly wouldn't have lost anything. After 70 or 80 brief years on earth, a time of mingled sorrows and joys, the atheist and the Christian alike would lie in the cold, dark ground for a very long time . . . like forever.

On the other hand, if God does exist, and if believing in Him and trusting in Him for salvation means an eternity in God's glorious kingdom someday, then the person who *doesn't* choose to believe has lost literally everything–while the Christian's true existence would only have just begun!

So I asked these sincere university members: "Which would you choose? The desolation of atheism or the possibility of the joy of being forever with a God who designed and loves you?" These hardened minions of the communist state said to me: "Dr. Finley, of course we would choose the latter."

We had a wonderful time of fellowship then, discussing the great philosophers down through the ages who acknowledged the need for God. Philosophers and psychologists have confessed to this reality: "Man does better if he acts as though God is there." The brilliant Voltaire once observed: "If God did not exist, it would be necessary to invent Him." Because, deep within the human heart, there's this sense that there must be more to life than just surviving and then dying.

It's interesting that discussing the existence of God within the framework of astronomy brings some fundamental questions into play. The sincere evolutionary scientist will propose that, given enough eons of years, it is possible for that one-in-a-billion flash of a spark of life to occur on one out of billions of planets and stars. And so here we are. In Biology 101, we are told: "Life begets life, but non-living things do not produce living things." But the evolutionist counters that, given enough time, yes, it *will* happen! Life can somehow come from non-life.

I remember picking up my messages at the front desk of a hotel in Orlando where I had been staying for a few weeks while doing an extended series of gospel meetings. By now I had a nodding acquaintance with some of the hotel staff. One day, as I was standing in the lobby, one of them said to me: "You're a preacher, aren't you?"

I guess it must show, and there's no reason to deny it, so I said, "Yes."

He then had something to say to me. "You've been here at the hotel for a couple of weeks now, and I've been wanting to tell you something." He wasn't defiant, but there was just a trace of "in your face" to his demeanor. Then he blurted it out: "Look, I'm an atheist."

I looked right at him. "You know what? I'd be an atheist too, but I just don't have enough faith. You have more faith than I do. Since I have to go by logic and don't have enough faith, I really can't be an atheist." I began to walk across the hotel lobby, and he called after me. "Hey, preacher, come back here. What in the world are you talking about?"

We sat down and I said to him: "Look, frankly I admire people who have faith like you, people who can make that 'quantum leap.'"

"What do you mean?"

I said, "Did you take biology? It says, 'life begets life,' but you believe that non-living things can eventually produce living things." I explained to him that, even back to the 1960s, high-speed computers were able to calculate the odds of whether or not the trial-and-error of Darwinian evolutionary progress could lead to the existence of life and the human race. Their conclusion: *zero*. There was basically no chance of it working, no matter how long you let the time scale run.

In their book, *How Now Shall We Live?* Chuck Colson and Nancy Pearcey quote from astronomer Sir Fred Hoyle, who put the odds of there being "life-by-chance" at one in ten to the fiftieth power. Then, to put it in perspective, he observed that it would be akin to giving that many blind people each a Rubik's cube puzzle (remember those?) and having all of them solve it at the exact same moment. Others use the tongue-in-cheek metaphor of an explosion in a print shop producing a perfect and complete dictionary. (*Now How Shall We Live?*, p. 74)

In addition, the idea that mutations can, over eons, slowly produce new and better life forms is contradicted by all that we see in the world of science around us. Colson and Pearcey further observe that mutations are somewhat like typos in a term paper. Yes, they occur, but they don't make the paper better, they make it worse! They are aberrations, not improvements. "Most mutations are harmful, often lethal to the organism" they write, "so that if mutations were to accumulate, the result would more likely be *de*volution than evolution" (Ibid. p. 85). Where can we point to a mutation in the human experience—a new appendage, say—that was a true improvement on what we had before? They also share the story of Francis Schaeffer, the Christian apologist, who posed this question. "Suppose a fish evolves lungs? What happens next? Does it move up to the next evolutionary stage? Of course not; It drowns." (Ibid. p. 87)

Michael Behe, professor of biochemistry at Lehigh University, wrote a 1993 book entitled *Darwin's Black Box*. He suggests the difficulty of a mousetrap "evolving" over millions of years. What is needed for a successful mousetrap?: a box, a wooden platform, a trip hammer, the spring. It wouldn't be possible to have just the bare box, catch a few mice . . . wait a few centuries . . . have the hammer "show up" . . . catch a few more mice . . . tear a few million more years off the calendar sheets . . . celebrate the sudden appearance of the spring. No, for a mousetrap to work, it has to come into existence all at once, most likely from the creative hands of a master designer. (from *How Now Shall We Live?*, p. 88)

As we discussed these challenges to the atheistic thinking of this sincere young hotel employee, he kept shaking his head in bewilderment. "Man, I need to look at this again. I never thought of all that."

In all candor, though, our greatest concern isn't what we might see or not see in a gleaming, well-funded laboratory or discover under the magnifying glass. A much larger issue is the void in a person's heart. What happens to people when they decide there is no God to love them? What happens to a society that determines there is no God in the heavens to look down upon the affairs of men?

As the Lord has sent us to the far-flung corners of the world to share His message of love, both of us have witnessed firsthand the effects of godlessness. In the Soviet system, under communism, we were told that the average Russian woman had three abortions by the time she was 40; some, as many as ten. Alcoholism was off the charts. Suicide rates were sky-high.

In a tragicomic kind of way, it was almost amusing to watch citizens go out of their way to be disobedient to Soviet rules. After communism began to collapse and it was less of a police state than before, people would take perverse delight in something as simple as driving without wearing their seatbelts. "*Nyet!* They can't make us!" was the typical response–even to a piece of legislation clearly designed for their own good.

The question of "law" has been one of profound and lively debate through the centuries. C. S. Lewis did some very helpful writing about it in the first portion of his three-part book, *Mere Christianity*. People everywhere, he writes, have an inner sense of a right and a wrong. When torn between two instincts, we usually know within our souls that one of them is more correct than the other. There is something "above" us all, a kind of Real Morality, and our standards either conform to it or fail to.

A scientist, Lewis suggests, could observe that gravity makes stones fall and that the earth rotates around the sun. In such a case, "law" is simply what we can see actually happening.

In only one case—that of man—do we see not only what we (and each other) are doing, we are also inwardly aware of this Higher Calling which we know we ought to do but where we usually fail. (*Mere Christianity*, p. 33)

In fact, even when the atheist cries out about the senseless unfairness of the world, he gives himself away. "My argument against God," Lewis writes, referring to when he, too, was an atheist, "was that the universe seemed so cruel and unjust. But how had I got this idea of *just* and *unjust?* A man does not call a line crooked unless he has some idea of a straight line. What was I comparing this universe with when I called it unjust? If the whole show was bad and senseless from A to Z, so to speak, why did I, who was supposed to be part of the show, find myself in such violent reaction against it?" (Ibid. p. 45)

In any case, it was right during this time when I was invited to visit the Russian city of Pushna, which is about 100 miles from Moscow. This is a fascinating place, for years off-limits to all foreigners. At the height of the Cold War, under Nikita Khrushchev, the city became a center for biological scientists. Thousands of brilliant men and women in their white lab coats settled there and worked for the Soviet state. Now, in the early 1990s, I was very eager to dialogue with these visionary citizens. The lecture hall was filled with at least a thousand of them, and, as agreed, they had selected the three topics for discussion: 1. Does God Exist? 2. Is the Bible True? 3. Who is Jesus Christ?

Night by night, I would speak for about 45 minutes, and then respond to various questions they had written out for me to consider. I wasn't concerned about the lectures, but anticipating the questions had me a bit concerned. After all, I was going to be facing some of the top brains in the world. And while you can plan a lecture, you can't plan those questions!

To my amazement, after three nights of intense meetings, I hadn't faced a single question on science. Not one. Not one question on atheism, either. Instead, these searching people asked questions like: How do you pray? If God is so good, then why is the world so bad? How can you have a better marriage? How do you forgive people who have hurt you?

By the end of our three-evening symposium, I felt like I really knew this audience quite well. I had been speaking to them, answering their questions, meeting with little groups of scientists. So finally I said to them: "You folks have really surprised me. I'm standing in the midst of some of the brightest minds in the world and you don't ask me one question about science. Not one question about atheism. Why?"

One of the scientists rose to his feet to give me an answer. I'd never in my life heard something like what he said. "Pastor Finley," he confessed, "for forty years, we tried atheism, and it failed. We all know that it failed. We saw firsthand how it left all of us morally barren; we were left with no hope, no future. So the question to us is not whether atheism is the answer to the question of life. We know all too well that it is not. No, our question is rather whether Christianity *is*. See, you don't have to answer all the questions about atheism; we just want to know that Christianity is the most viable option."

I had a spiritual thrill go through me as I saw how our loving God had already prepared them to accept His offer. After those decades of godless existence, these precious people had a hunger in their hearts for something more. They recognized that there was something lacking. As Augustine once put it, "There is a God-shaped vacuum inside each of us." Then he added, "And Lord, our hearts will never find rest until they find rest in You."

In *Mere Christianity*, Lewis writes that men have always tried vainly to find happiness outside of God, apart from Him. "And out of that hopeless attempt has come nearly all that we call human history—money, poverty, ambition, war, prostitution, classes, empires, slavery—the long terrible story of man trying to find something other than God which will make him happy. The reason why it can never succeed is this. God made us: invented us as a man invents an engine. A car is made to run on gasoline, and it would not run properly on anything else. Now God designed the human machine to run on Himself." (*Mere Christianity*, p. 53, 54)

And every other plan we try–whether it's atheism, communism, or the selfish *isms* in our own neighborhoods--goes awry in the end. It works for a while and then fizzles out. "The machine conks" is how Lewis puts it.

We believe that most of the lonely people all around us are like those laboratory wizards living in Pushna. They're not swayed so much by arguments from science or deep philosophy; their consideration of atheism is prompted more by personal despair. Like that young woman Shawn met on the plane. Awful things had happened to her. Unexplained tragedies had come into her life. She described in stark emotional terms how she had been deeply wounded as a child. And when she unleashed her anger in front of her own minister, he had no answers to share.

A couple will grieve when their little baby is born dead. "God *couldn't* exist; how could He do a thing like this to us?" they demand in their grief. People look at the wars, the injustices, the tsunamis and the earthquakes that devour, and cry out: "God couldn't exist." Elie Wiesel, observing the horrors of the Holocaust, once said in bitterness: "Why doesn't God resign and let someone more competent take His place?"

What these good people need, as they cope with their disappointments, is not merely evidence that God exists, but an experience in their own hearts and lives. They need a personal encounter with Him; they need to meet a Friend named Jesus who can not only create a world, but can also create a new life for them. When this miracle happens, when a life is changed, that surely is the greatest evidence for the existence of a loving God.

Several years ago I was preaching up in Massachusetts, near my New England roots. One night a young man attended who was the head of a motorcycle gang. Bucky had been in and out of prison scores of times; he had scars all over his face. And there he was with many of his fellow gang members. I was astonished and thrilled when he came forward and accepted Jesus as his Savior. In fact, a number of his fellow motorcycle buddies walked down the aisle with him.

These were hard-core tough guys. Bucky told me personally how he used to go out on Saturday nights, get half-drunk, then take a beer bottle, break it on a wall and go stick somebody in the face with it. He indulged in this kind of sadism for the pure, *fallen* joy it gave him. So he truly was a changed man now.

One evening I was chatting with him. He was still an intimidating presence, standing a good 6'2", rippling with tattooed muscles. He still had his leather jacket, boots and beard, and his face was lined with deep scars. I was glad I didn't have to be afraid of him any more! He had now accepted Christ, he was a new creation . . . and I believed that. On this particular evening, a middle-aged businessman came up and almost accosted me. He began to argue vehemently against the existence of God. He was actually a bright fellow—and he knew it. He thought he was so smart, so intelligent, and who was I to contradict his convictions? He literally poked a finger in my face as the pitch of his voice rose higher and higher.

I confess: I was a bit tired and worn out that evening. It had been a long day, filled with appointments and a very full church service that night. I shot a peek over at Bucky and caught his eye. *Could you give me a little help* is what my glance said to him. My new motorcycle friend, swelling up to his full 6'2", still smelling of motor oil and with all the Harley-Davidson confidence in the world, strolled over. He towered over my obnoxious little critic and said to him: "Sir, if this were six months ago, I would've taken you out in a back alley for insulting a good friend of mine like that. I'd have busted you up good. So you better be glad that there *is* a God, because He changed my life. So now I just want to hug you, and then you can tell Pastor Finley you're sorry." And with that, he reached out, tattoos and all, and smothered that little businessman in a bear hug.

Certainly the most powerful testimony, the most important changed heart . . . is the one that beats in our own chest. Both of us can raise our hands high and give an It Is Written confession that Jesus Christ moved on our own hearts and made us into new men. That's all the evidence that *we* need! And since then we've both had the incredible experience of working with thousands of people, watching them come out of witchcraft, atheism, prison, battle-scarred existences—and begin to believe in God. It's amazing what God can do!

No, we still can't put "God" in a test tube and analyze the divine DNA. Just as we can't measure in a laboratory vial how much we love our wives. An onlooker might look at the external evidence: how much time we spend with them, how we speak to them and treat them. But that's not really quantitative, scientific evidence that can be calibrated on a graph.

Perhaps the existence of God is a little like that. When we look for absolute proof—the kind that would completely satisfy the scientific method—maybe we're trying to empirically quantify something that can't be quantified. Maybe, when we do that, we're trying to measure the Infinite in terms of ounces, grams, or gallons. But frankly, no matter how hard you try, our Almighty God just doesn't fit into a test tube.

But that doesn't mean we don't have evidence! The apostle Paul reminds us in the book of Romans that we have plenty of it. *For since the creation of the world His invisible attributes are clearly seen, being understood by the things that are made, even His eternal power and Godhead, so that they are without excuse.* (Romans 1:20)

According to the Bible, there's enough evidence that nobody really has a legitimate excuse for not noticing the existence of God. And if you really want to come face to face with Him, take a quiet moment and examine your own heart, because there is a divine spark there that confirms, beyond the shadow of a doubt, that we are more than just carbon-based life forms.

But it does take that search, that willingness to look at a sunset and see more than pastel reds and clouds scudding into darkness. In his book, *Believe in Miracles But Trust in Jesus,* Adrian Rogers once talked to a man whose marriage was on the rocks. He wanted help; he needed counseling. But when Rogers asked him, "Are you a Christian?", the man laughed scornfully. "No way. I'm an atheist."

Interestingly, Pastor Rogers gave him the Budapest treatment! "Would it be generous to say that you know half of all that there is to know?" Well, the man calmed down and admitted that that would be extremely generous!

"All right then," Rogers suggested, "how do you know that God does not exist in the other half of the knowledge that you do not know?" So the man conceded that, well, he was really more of an agnostic, a doubter.

"Are you an honest doubter?" Rogers wanted to know. "Are you willing to sincerely look at the evidence?" He pointed out that a "dishonest doubter" doesn't find God for the same reason most thieves never find a policeman, they aren't looking very hard!

Well, this gentleman admitted that if he had to be a doubter, he'd like to be an honest one. So he agreed to play by Rogers' rules, to go home and carefully study the Gospel of John. In fact, he signed a "waiver," promising to follow and commit his life to whatever plain truth God might show him in those few pages.

A few weeks later, that same man, with his arrogance and anger melted away, came back to the pastor's office, fell on his knees, burst into tears, and accepted Jesus Christ as his own Savior. (*Believe in Miracles But Trust in Jesus*, pp. 200-203) All along, he had felt some unexplainable tug on his heart, a desire for something eternal. The Bible says: *He has made everything beautiful in its time. Also He has put eternity in their hearts.* (Ecclesiastes 3:11)

And friend, God has planted eternity in *your* heart as well. There is something in there right now that calls you to reach beyond yourself.

You may be one of those who has experienced more than your share of disappointment. You've suffered the kinds of crushing blows that make you doubt. And maybe you've been let down by people who call themselves Christians.

But stop to think about it. Why is it you still have such an ache in your heart to know that God exists? Why is it that your disappointment is so, well, disappointing?

It's because you were *born* with eternity in your heart! There's a part of you that longs to reach out for God's hand and find out that He's really still there. And today, this moment as you read these lines . . . would be the perfect time to take that chance.

PRAYER

Father in heaven, thank You for being our Designer, our Creator, and our Friend. But so many, Lord, have lost their sight of You. You know who they are and where they are. Thank You so much that in the context of our struggles, our disappointments, our deepest sorrows and greatest griefs—You're still there. You understand when we doubt. You love us still, even in our dark and questioning moments. You remain by our side even then. You're there to give us that ray of hope, that spark of encouragement. And so, Lord, today, when somebody is struggling with Your existence, battling their pain, their sorrow, their tears, help them right now to take that step of faith. Help them right now to reach out their hand to grasp Yours. In Jesus' name we pray, Amen.

CHAPTER TWO

Is the Bible God's Word?

Two grizzled prospectors were traveling with a large stash of gold secreted in their belongings when they suddenly found themselves without a place to stay for the night. As the gloom and chill of evening crept over them, they noticed some lights in the trees and discovered a little cabin.

"Excuse us," they asked the owner, "but we don't have any place to stay. Could we stay here, just for tonight?"

"You can stay here as long as you need to," the man graciously replied. And with that, two tired and grateful travelers turned in for the night. It occurred to them, however, that they should safeguard all that gold they were carrying.

"Why don't we take turns sleeping," one of them said, lowering his voice, "so that the other can stand guard?"

"Oh, that's a good idea," his partner agreed. "I'll go first."

He sat on the edge of his bed for a long time as the minutes crept by. Even though it was very late now, a pale light continued to shine around the edges of the bedroom door, and he could hear faint noises coming from the other side.

"I wonder what he's doing," the self-appointed guard thought to himself. Curiosity getting the better of him, he crept over and opened the door just a crack, peering into the living room.

Their host was sitting at a table by the fire, with his Bible open, his hands folded in prayer. Quietly, the prospector closed the door and said to his partner, "Listen, I think we can both go to bed now, because we're staying in the house of an honest man."

Does it make a difference what a person reads? If that man had been reading the *Wall Street Journal*, or a tawdry novel, or a so-called "men's magazine," would it have inspired the same kind of confidence?

Even in the postmodern, 21st century world we live in, there is something about the Bible that inspires trust. It still holds a special place in many people's hearts. In fact, for millions, the Bible is more than just a good bit of reading or a masterpiece of sacred literature or the literary lockbox that protects a weary miner's gold from predators. They believe it is literally the Word of God. But is it? Do these claims hold up? Can they be believed today? Do the latest scientific and archeological discoveries undercut this Book the people of God have always believed in?

The Bible itself claims the status of being God's Word—so if a skeptic wanted to reject its divinity and simply admire the literature and noble ideals of this Book, he would be endeavoring to appreciate a mountain of admitted falsehoods! In Isaiah 40:8, the Bible plainly says: *The grass withers, the flower fades, but the Word of our God stands forever.* In other words, this Book, "the Word of our God," is an eternal gift. Its truths will never fade away or become obsolete. In three thousand different places, the Bible proclaims its own inspiration. Time after time, great truths are preceded by: "The Lord said" or "God said." So to reject the inspiration of the Bible is to reject at least three thousand statements of the Bible itself.

God's Word also boldly defends its status of being

inspired *in toto,* or from beginning to end, Genesis to Revelation. II Timothy 3:16, 17 says: *All Scripture is given by inspiration of God, and is profitable for doctrine, for reproof, for correction, for instruction in righteousness, that the man of God may be complete, thoroughly equipped for every good work.* Christians rightly proclaim the doctrine of *Sola Scriptura*—"The Bible and the Bible only"—but we are equally called to embrace *Omnis Scriptura*—"ALL of the Bible." If it is truly inspired, then we can't "pick and choose" depending on our personal whims and tastes!

It is an amazing thing to discover that this ancient Book was penned by 44 different writers, filling up 66 unique "books," and that this was done over the span of 1,500 years. Some of these men were great spiritual leaders like Moses and Paul. Luke was a doctor. But Peter and John were simple fishermen! All of them were sinners. King David was an adulterer and a murderer. And yet there is a cohesive unity to the Bible, a consistent thread of truth, a divine "stamp."

It is written in II Peter 1:20, 21: *No prophecy of Scripture is of any private interpretation, for prophecy never came by the will of man, but holy men of God spoke as they were moved* [or "carried along," says another version] *by the Holy Spirit.* So the Bible is not a human book, but a divine one! It is literally God's letter, His message of love to a lost human race.

But what does it mean, then, when the Word of God describes itself as "inspired," that it is "given by inspiration of God"? Music lovers everywhere sit in awe every Christmas when they hear Handel's beloved *Messiah* performed, and then read that he composed the entire masterpiece in just twenty-four days. "He must have been inspired," they conclude. Students of science muse that Albert Einstein surely was "inspired" when he discovered that $e = mc^2$.

And yes, there have been many moments for both of us when the Lord gave us a powerful impulse that led to a new sermon, or suddenly moved us to pray earnestly for a hurting friend. You awaken at two in the morning with this thrilling insight, and you want to turn on the lamp and scribble it down, fearing it will be gone before sunup. Is that inspiration? Is it from God? Well, yes, to both questions. But there is a difference between what the Holy Spirit might do through our pens just now or through Mr. Handel in the year 1741, and what heaven moved to do through the 66 books we find in the Holy Bible. Christians believe that the inspiration of Scriptures was a singular, clear-cut, supernatural process that is unique. Despite our prayers and times of communion with heaven, books from Boonstra/Finley will always be simply "human inspiration," not divine.

And divine inspiration is authoritative! Divine inspiration is when God paints a panoramic picture through a vision or a dream. Oftentimes in the Bible, God moved directly upon the mind of a man. King David once said, in II Samuel 23:2: *"The Spirit of the Lord spoke by me, And His word was on my tongue."* The Old Testament prophets like Hosea and Jeremiah and Joel prefaced their messages of warning and encouragement in this way. Even in cases where a Bible writer compiled historical records, or wrote out answers to issues and problems facing the Church, or drew from the writings of earlier Bible authors—as Luke did—or even employed the aid of secretaries or scribes, like Paul, God's inspiring Spirit was present in a miraculous way, safeguarding the process.

It is plain as we read one Bible book to the next that God didn't dictate every word! The human vocabulary, the personality, the unique spiritual gifts and perspectives that one particular writer had, and not another, are fascinating to discover. But despite the "fishermen" moments that show through, the different colors of thread used, the overall fabric and mosaic are amazingly consistent.

By the time of Christ, 2000 years ago, the 39 books of the Old Testament had essentially been accepted as "canonical," as being God's Word. But it's sometimes said by new Bible students, "All right, the OT is Scripture. I can accept that. However, here in the New Testament, people are simply quoting back from the Old Testament. Maybe the New Testament is just man's word, then."

But consider the reality that the four Gospels, for example, were written by Matthew, Mark, Luke, and John . . . as four face-to-face encounters with Jesus Christ. These disciples had been with Jesus and had heard and experienced these miracles and teachings with their own eyes and ears. The apostle Paul, of course, was dramatically converted on the road to Damascus (see Acts 9). This was a heavenly confrontation that was literally blinding! So throughout the New Testament, we are blessed to have firsthand, reliable histories, inspired by the Holy Spirit, of these encounters with Jesus. And remember, this passage which emphatically declares "All scripture" to be inspired, is IN the New Testament! So on both sides of the Cross, we find a powerful unity, an integrated wholeness to all of Scripture.

It's encouraging that Bible writers themselves grappled with some of these very same questions, and yet swore their unswerving allegiance to the Word. In Peter's second epistle, he addresses the letters written by his fellow author, Paul. In them, there are "some things hard to understand," he confesses. There are those who take the difficult trains of thought, the apparent contradictions, and "twist to their own destruction." But clearly Peter was affirming the inspiration of the New Testament books. He talks about Paul's writing along with "the *rest* of the Scriptures."

But this takes God's people today to a most challenging issue. Picture Peter, rough, uneducated fixer of fishing nets that he was . . . and now the author of inspired books. Matthew, the tax man, wrote his Gospel before the invention of TurboTax software and the great mathematical discoveries of the past twenty centuries. The author of Job wrote about the stars and constellations in a bygone era before our Hubble telescopes and Voyager space modules explored the heavens.

In addition, the "Indiana Jones" explorers of modern times continue to unearth fresh scrolls, new artifacts and treasures and historical troves. Don't they render these 66 dusty books obsolete? Do the claims of the Bible fall apart? Isn't God's Word doomed as an authoritative guide when scientific and literary discoveries go marching on?

Incredibly, the very opposite is true! The spade of the modern archeologist is actually the Bible's best friend. The more Bible students today explore biblical archeology, the more we confirm the authenticity of Scripture. Just within the last century—actually, between 1932 and 1938—a new series of letters was discovered. These "Lachish Letters," uncovered in southern Israel, dated clear back to Babylonian times.

Archeological experts used a number of techniques to confirm their dating with precise accuracy. And these documents, unearthed about 24 miles north of Beersheba, corroborate Babylon's attacks on the city of Jerusalem. Going back to the year 586 B.C., this is secular confirmation of something Christians have read about in Chronicles and the prophetic book of Daniel.

A discovery in Jordan, circa 1848, has come to be known as the "Moabite Stone." Carved indelibly into the rock is an account of Moabite attacks on Israel, perfectly consistent with the biblical record.

Another powerful beam of new light came about two centuries ago. For a long time, secular historians had doubted the Bible stories regarding the "Hittites." Genesis 10 describes them as being a nation founded by Canaan, a grandson of Noah. They're mentioned in the Bible a total of 47 times, but there was nothing in the secular history books to back that up. Scholars scoffed at the notion and belittled the "blind faith" of Christians who continued to believe that such a group of people group existed.

But then in July of 1799, during an invasion of Egypt by Napoleon, he took with him a team of nearly three thousand artisans and scholars. They did some digging in a delta area by a town called Rashid, or Rosetta, and came upon a large, black basalt slab. Today we know it, of course, as the Rosetta Stone. Many visitors to the British Museum have seen it on display.

This smooth, dark piece of stone was covered with writing in three languages. One was Greek, which Egyptian rulers like Ptolemy V were using in 196 B.C., the time of the stone's creation. So that was easily translated. The second language was called "demotic," which simply meant the "common script" of Egypt. It was a cursive style of writing, used mostly for secular documents.

Then there was a third language, a mysterious form of hieroglyphics. The Egyptians had used such picture markings for thousands of years, but it now seemed a lost art. What did they say? Who could translate?

For two decades the meaning stayed hidden. But a British physicist named Thomas Young, and then later a brilliant French Egyptologist named Jean Francois Champollion managed to decipher the "Coptic" origins of the hieroglyphics. Comparing word-by-word with the Greek and the flowing demotic prose, Champollion was able to unravel the mystery. And even though the writing was originally done by Egyptian priests to honor the exploits of the pharaoh, the hieroglyphics also confirmed some fierce battles between Egypt and . . . the Hittites! Today there's really not a modern scholar in the world who disbelieves the Hittites. In fact, numerous Hittite city ruins have been discovered in modern-day Turkey. So the Bible is indeed proved—not disproved—by archeology.

Sometimes ancient Bible prophecies combine with today's current Holy Land "digs" to renew our faith in God's sure Word. Ancient writers often penned their messages on round cylinders. There is an artifact displayed in the British Museum called the "Cyrus Cylinder." Here is the story.

In Isaiah 44:28 we read a promise concerning the children of Israel who were suffering in Babylonian captivity. The prophet Isaiah, writing a good *150 years before* the birth of Cyrus, pens this amazing prediction: *"[I am the Lord] who says of Cyrus, 'He is my shepherd, And he shall perform all My pleasure. Even saying to Jerusalem, "You shall be built," and to the temple, "Your foundation shall be laid."'"*

These words were written in approximately 700 B.C., but not fulfilled until the year 539 B.C., a century and a half later! Cyrus wasn't even born when Isaiah was moved to make the divine prediction and mention him by name.

Here is how this Bible prophecy was fulfilled. Cyrus, this king of Persia bent on attacking Babylon, moved his armies into position and then realized he couldn't proceed. Inside the walled fortress, the Babylonians had a twenty-year supply of food, and the River Euphrates ran right through the center of this beautiful capital city, giving the kingdom a constant water supply. The walls of the city were allegedly so wide that two chariots could race side by side along the top! The place was absolutely impregnable, so how could this bold prediction by Isaiah ever come to pass?

In a brilliant and unexpected move, Cyrus' armies surreptitiously diverted the Euphrates River into newly dug reservoirs. On the night of the infamous drunken feast, described in Daniel 5, Belshazzar's generals were all in a stupor as the water levels quietly went down. The armies of Persia were able to easily walk right through the riverbed and into the unprotected mecca.

Now here is the remarkable thing. The "Cyrus Cylinder," in the London museum, describes this very attack! Cyrus is mentioned by name, and the report confirms that this wise and gracious victor willingly permitted the captives of Israel to go free to rebuild their temple.

A huge treasure trove of tablets came to light as recently as 1964. Located at "Tell Mardikh" in northern Syria, a 148-acre patch of land has yielded something like 15,000 tablets and ancient documents written in ancient Sumerian script, dating back to very early Bible times. Professor Giovanni Pettinato, the epigrapher working for the University of Rome, soon found that literally hundreds of personal names were included, as well as historical details.

The lives and experiences of Abraham and Isaac are mentioned. Most compelling of all was the confirmation of the existence of a number of biblical towns like Ashdod, Sidon, Lachish, Megiddo, Gaza, Sinai, Ashtaroth, Sodom, Gomorrah, Joppa, Damascus, and even a place called Urusalima (Jerusalem).

Detailed legal codes were spelled out in minute detail, shattering the typical criticism that Bible records of the complicated Mosaic law in Leviticus must have been a fabrication. One secular web site concludes its report with this frank confession: "The Ebla tablets are important because they includes the names of cities and people that appear in the Old Testament, and therefore provide evidence for the historical accuracy of the Bible" (*www.digonsite.com*)

Careful researchers also point to the Dead Sea scrolls, unrolling to an incredible 54 feet of painstaking writing. Sir Frederick Kenyon, a foremost archeologist and Bible student, has said that any Christian can take up the Bible and know with utmost confidence that this truly *is* the Word of God.

So the pickax and the looking glass of the honest archeologist tend to give support to the Christian's faith. Does archeology absolutely *prove* the Bible? No. It confirms; it doesn't prove. There will always be questions, because the Word of God is an infinite and miraculous message, and we are finite people. We will always have questions. There will be things we don't understand until we sit as students at the feet of Jesus. At times we have to humbly bow and recognize that an apparent contradiction is not going to be answered *today*.

MARK: When I was a young college student, I went to a theology professor of mine, a wise and humble man named Mel Clemons. "Pastor Clemons," I asked, "why is it that there are contradictions in the Bible?" I should have said *apparent* contradictions, but he was kind enough to still answer my query. He sagely replied, "Mark, do you know what I do with what appear to be contradictions in the Bible?"

"No," I said.

"I have a little jar in my mind," he explained. "And every time I come across an apparent contradiction, I just put it on a little scroll, a mental scroll, and I put it in the jar of my mind. Then I go on. I keep studying. I keep trusting. I keep learning. And do you know what happens? I'm studying the Bible, say, three or four weeks later, and as I read something new, I'm able to take the cap off that jar and take that one mental scroll out, and I cross it off. 'Now I understand,' I say. Because it was only an *apparent* contradiction."

After hearing that wonderful testimony, I've sometimes wanted to say to my own questioners: "I'd rather know all that I know, and not know all that I don't know . . . than to know all I don't know and not know what I know!" In other words, I would rather know all of the things that I do know about God and His Word and not know the things that aren't yet plain to me, than to cast out and reject all of my certainties, the things that are wonderfully plain in the Bible, and base my life on the uncertainties that still exist.

Shawn and I, for example, as young Christians were perplexed by the fact that in the gospel of Matthew, you can read a genealogy of Jesus Christ, and then in Luke's writings, it is quite a different list! Why? Is one of them a mistake? What should we do?

As time went on, however, and the Spirit continued to guide, we made the same discovery as many fellow believers. Matthew, we find, traced the lineage of Joseph, Jesus' legal father, and especially focused on the royal line of the house of David. Luke, by contrast, emphasized the actual blood line going through Christ's mother, Mary. The good news is that these two varying accounts help us to see our Savior not only as the promised Covenant Child, but also as a full-fledged part of the human race! Jesus truly is the second Adam.

As God's people continue to trust and grow, we find that really, there's adequate evidence to believe in the Bible. A favorite author puts it this way: "God never asks us to believe, without giving sufficient evidence upon which to base our faith. His existence, His character, the truthfulness of His word, are all established by testimony that appeals to our reason; and this testimony is abundant. Yet God has never removed the possibility of doubt. Our faith must rest upon evidence, not demonstration. Those who wish to doubt will have opportunity; while those who really desire to know the truth will find plenty of evidence on which to rest their faith." (*Steps To Christ*, p. 105)

But there's one common objection that well-meaning friends sometimes raise—and when you are preaching on television or in an extensive satellite evangelistic series, it is a most pertinent question. That is, "Doesn't the Bible go out of its way to burnish and promote the Christian story? Isn't it slanted to glorify that movement, to make everyone in it look better than they really were? We can't trust a book if it's blatant propaganda."

That's a good question! Any preacher who counts the cars in the church parking lot would like to see more vehicles there than there really are. We'd all like to announce baptism figures in the thousands instead of the tens. So is God's Word filled with a lot of public relations "puff pieces" that cannot be verified or believed?

The answer is a simple one. Does Moses look very good where he impulsively and foolishly kills a man? Does King David look very good where he lusts on the rooftop that hot summer night and then commits adultery with the wife of a trusted soldier? And then conspires to have him killed? Do the sons of Jacob look very good in the eyes of the community when they lie and cheat their neighbors and slaughter all the Shechemites?

How about Peter? Waving a sword, he boasted to Jesus and the other disciples about what a stout defender he would be, then the very same night denied his Lord three times. This is the same Peter who unwisely wanted to "walk on water," and promptly sank like a stone. He might well have pleaded later with authors Matthew, Mark, Luke, and John, "Do you have to include these stories? Can't you skip over them?"

But there they are, with all the shameful details and sordid colors. The entire story of the children of Israel is one long, sad saga of shallow, self-serving disobedience. God's people would fall into sin, and prophets would call them to repentance. It's a never-ending cycle, and certainly not one that glosses over problems.

Isn't this, then, evidence of the Bible's truthfulness? We mentioned those Egyptian hieroglyphics—now, *they* were propaganda masterpieces! Have you ever seen a fat, overweight pharaoh in one of those paintings or carvings? No, the various "Ramses" were always handsome, strong, mighty, "buff" men of valor, almost demi-gods. Any artisan portraying a pharaoh with a pot belly would soon have found himself sleeping among the sphinxes! But the Bible gives us a real picture of human struggles, of our joys and sorrows, foibles and failings. Why? Because God inspired true accounts and accurate stories, told for our benefit and encouragement.

So when we come to God's Word with our questions and our needy hearts, what do we do? We can only trust in the Bible when we read it with an open mind and a prayerful heart. But why read it at all? True, seeing their host read it gave emotional comfort and a few hours of contented sleep to those two gold miners. But what is there in the Bible for us today? What was God's ultimate purpose in giving us this gift?

Most of us could look through our photo albums and recall a favorite romantic love story that is our very own. I like to remember a college year when I left the comforts of the United States and went to be a student missionary in faraway Brazil. I was really in the jungles! Back in those "dark ages," there weren't any Internet cafes where you could stay connected to your girlfriend back home. No phone cards that offered U.S. calls for eight cents a minute. You might as well be on the moon.

In the ministry years since then, I've been around the globe and said more goodbyes than I care to remember or recount, but this was my first time away from family and friends. And I keenly missed one person in particular: "Teenie." She's now my wife, but during those long months, she was just a pretty photo in my wallet. How I treasured the occasional trips back to the port city of Belém. That was where the mailbox was! That was where the love letters were waiting. That was where a young man in love could stay connected to the object of his desires.

The Bible is truly a love letter, a *Word* to us from God. Yes, our heavenly Father would love to communicate with us face to face, to walk with us and talk with us in the Garden, just like in Eden. But because we are separated from heaven by a wall of sin, God impressed the minds of His prophets; He directed them to write down and share the message of His love, to reassure us through all time. That's really what the Bible is all about. The reason we need the Bible is because we're separated from face-to-face communication. And so it is in these writings that God reveals Himself.

It's a wonderful moment when the Lord moves a person's heart in the midnight hour and gives them a helpful sermon idea. What a blessing when a Christian musician feels the Spirit's quiet presence and composes a masterpiece that changes lives. You may be driving along on the freeway, and suddenly just *know* that God wants you to visit a certain discouraged friend. Who knows, you might even be one of the fortunate few who has an encounter with an angel of light.

But friend, all of these messages and impulses, holy as they might be, are to be subjected to THE authority of God's holy Word. The Bible is the last word, the court of highest appeal. It is the "trump" that supersedes any other signal we might receive, any other conviction we might discover or think we believe.

C. S. Lewis once commented that Christians and atheists alike were prone to have their beliefs waver in the breeze. Something as simple as a good (or bad) meal or a night in an uncomfortable bed might change what we think! How important, then, to focus on the reliable Word of God on a regular basis, to "train the habit of Faith." (*Mere Christianity*, p. 124)

To read the Bible carefully and daily, as we're encouraged to do, just like the "infant" Christians in Berea. In Acts 17:11 it is written: *They received the word with all readiness, and searched the Scriptures daily to find out whether these things were so.*

What a comfort it is to know that this great old Book is true, ever true, and always true! It says today what it has always said. John 3:16 reads at this very moment the same as when Jesus said those words of salvation for the very first time: *"For God so loved the world . . ."*

Here at It Is Written, it has been wonderful to see the Bible transform lives. From Moscow to Malaysia to Michigan, it takes hurting sinners and makes them into new men and women for God's kingdom. And we know it is inspired because it inspires us when we read it! Our libraries are bulging over with other books—thousands of them—but we keep coming back to this one Book. There is something different about the Bible.

Many people know the infamous story of the "Mutiny on the Bounty." After Fletcher Christian and his fellow rebels put Captain Bligh overboard, they knew they had to flee from British justice. Together with a small number of captive Tahitian men and women, they set sail for a deserted, uncharted island and planned to make a new, permanent home there.

But three factors doomed them. First of all, there were more men than women—and this on an island they never planned to leave. Second, in a rash and disastrous moment, the Englishmen voted to divide the island only among themselves and force the Tahitian men into involuntary servitude. Third, they quickly discovered how to brew a whiskey from local tropical plants.

It took very little time for this island to become a veritable hell instead of a paradise. Because there were too few women, jealousy and promiscuous adultery were rampant. Tempers flared constantly, fueled by the steady flow of alcohol. One of the women, distraught with the sin and sorrow going on, flung herself from the cliffs. Now the man-to-woman ratio was even worse, and the troubles escalated.

In a final, violent bloodbath, the feuding men soon slaughtered one another. Soon just one man was left: a plain, ungifted deck hand named Alexander Smith.

Years later, a Captain Folger, commanding the American seal-hunting vessel, *Topaz*, happened upon the supposedly deserted island called Pitcairn. To his surprise, handsome young men and women greeted the vessel using the King's English. Here was a quiet, well-ordered community, filled with 35 clean, law-abiding citizens.

Why the change? Smith and the surviving women had found a Bible in Captain Bligh's sea trunk; the entire village began to read and study. Now the amazed visitors from outside their isolated world watched as children bowed their heads and gave thanks to God before their meals; each child old and young knew the Lord's Prayer by heart. Doors were left unlocked; beautiful young girls romped over the island, secure in the knowledge that they would not be harmed or molested (Caroline Alexander, *The Bounty*).

What a heartbreaking tragedy, to hear just recently that Pitcairn Island had set aside the Bible as its guide and safety net. In a scandal that reached into the faraway *Los Angeles Times*, it was reported in 2004 that men of the island were once again raping and abusing. Charges were filed against several, and it seemed that Paradise had once again slipped away, when the Word of God was lost to them.

The days of holiness earlier found in that faraway garden spot can be ours as well. When we open God's Book, it seems as if we are suddenly ushered into the presence of God Himself. In those quiet moments when, perhaps, the rest of the family has gone to bed, and we can sit alone by the fire or at our favorite study desk with an open Bible, it's as if Jesus is right there with us, opening up His Word as He did with His two grieving friends on the road to Emmaus. (See Luke 24:13-35)

Friend, no other book can do that. Any other can influence and guide and inform, but they cannot revolutionize our lives as only this Book can do. When we read God's love letter to us, something begins to happen in our heart. It changes us; it molds us into the character of Christ. The apostle Peter describes us as being "born again" by the Word of God.

But this journey of joy, this pilgrimage to the throne of heaven, can only begin when we take the first step. Maybe your own Bible has been collecting a lot of dust lately. Perhaps you feel a need today to deepen your study of God's Word, to make a commitment that you will be more faithful in your devotional life. There's no better time than now to make or renew that choice!

The first steps to eternity are just a heartbeat away.

PRAYER

Father, Your Word beckons to us. As long as it stays closed on our shelves, unused in the corner of our life, we'll never sense its inspiration. Father, help us to open to the Psalms and quietly read them. Lead us to the Gospels so that we may understand Jesus. May the Book that our mothers read to us become again the passion and the desire of our lives—to read and understand it. Father, You've never turned anybody away. We want to give You and Your message to us an honest chance just now. And so we commit ourselves to seeking, to study, to following You in Your Word. Enable us to do that today. In Jesus' name we pray, Amen.

CHAPTER *THREE*

Is Jesus God?

The landscape of history is decorated with the names of prominent people who have changed the way we think and live. Names like Aristotle and Plato fall from the lips of people who have never even read their books, because they have had such a profound impact on the development of human civilization.

Alexander the Great, Napoleon, Hitler, and others are remembered—in contrast—because of the way they tried to recolor the map with their military juggernauts.

Isaac Newton, Marie Curie, Galileo, Edison, and Einstein are mentioned in our history books for pushing back the frontiers of scientific knowledge.

But without a doubt, the name that towers above all the rest is Jesus of Nazareth. Nobody has ever had as much impact on human civilization as this humble Carpenter from Nazareth. Everyone recognizes Him as a good Man and a capable Teacher—but as much as one-third of the world falls to its knees and also reveres Him as God in the flesh.

So who was this Jesus of Nazareth? Was He really the Son of God? For nearly two thousand years, the world has struggled with the question of His identity. In a strange twist of irony, some of the recent voices of doubt have come directly from within the ranks of the Christian church!

The highly controversial Episcopal Bishop, John Shelby Spong, has written several books attacking the historic faith of the Church. In volumes like *Rescuing the Church From Fundamentalism* and *Why Christianity Must Change or Die*, he poses challenging questions that strike at the very heart of the Christian religion. He claims that the virgin birth, understood as literal biology, makes the divinity of Christ impossible. "All virgin birth stories, including the ones about Jesus," he writes, "were fully discredited as biological truths by the discovery in 1724 of the existence of an egg cell." He also claims that the resurrection of Jesus is impossible, and that the incarnation—Jesus existing with God from eternity before Bethlehem—is nothing but mythology. To continue to believe in such fables, he complains, requires a Christian to endure a "mental lobotomy."

Sadly, many have followed in his footsteps, including groups like the *Jesus Seminar*, a self-appointed Bible tribunal that "decides" the authenticity of Scriptural passages by voting on them. Robert W. Funk, the chair of the panel, wrote admiringly of one of Spong's books: "He gathers the anachronisms of traditional faith and nails them to the cross." And the end result of these efforts, always, is to call into question the divinity of Jesus. Was He really God?

Some in the church wonder if maybe this question is a whole lot of fuss about nothing. But they couldn't be further from the truth! If Jesus is not God, then all He can offer is a bit more moral ideology. And this in a world already awash in "theories" and self-help principles. Bookshelves at Barnes and Noble sag under the weight of a myriad of competing moral frameworks. As one Christian apologist pointed out, "A bit more makes no difference." If Jesus is just one more in a long line of good teachers, then He can't offer us the one thing we crave most: eternal life. All of Dr. Phil's advice or Oprah's recommendations can't extend your life beyond the grave by even half an hour.

What's more, even good teachers can't offer us the power to follow their teachings! Where is the power to change the prostitute, the drunkard, the hopelessly addicted, the man filled with materialism and godlessness? Only a Teacher who is also God could provide that.

How clearly does the Bible address the issue of Jesus Christ actually being God? The weekend Jesus died, two discouraged disciples were walking from Jerusalem to Emmaus. Their hopes were dashed; they were sure their world had come to an end. They had thought this Jesus was the Messiah, their hoped-for Savior who would set them free from Roman tyranny. But now He was dead. They had seen Him die with their own eyes. Even on that pivotal weekend, they had already succumbed to the existential despair of the "Jesus Seminar," deciding that miracles are impossible and resurrection just a hysterical female fantasy. They reflected on all they had heard Him say in three-and-a-half years, and now painfully asked themselves the question that is still being discussed now: "Who was this Man? Is it possible He could have been what He claimed?"

As they walked along in the gloom, a mysterious fellow Traveler joined them and entered into the discussion. Carefully, gently, He chided them for abandoning the very truths they had heard Him declare, the very promises that had been expounded in the Scriptures they claimed to love. *"O foolish ones, and slow of heart to believe in all that the prophets have spoken! Ought not the Christ to have suffered these things and to enter into His glory?" And beginning at Moses and all the Prophets, He expounded to them in all the Scriptures the things concerning Himself.* (Luke 24:25-27)

The good news is that the same amazing litany of fulfilled prophecies which brought renewed faith and confidence to those two disciples are still in God's Word for our encouragement today! Taken together, they provide supernatural proof that Jesus truly is God.

Most famous people who have biographies written about them see the books roll off the press either in the latter part of their life or well after their death. But not in the case of Jesus! No, His biography was essentially written before He was born.

The little Old Testament prophetic book of Micah was written 700 years before the events in Bethlehem. But here is what it says: *But you, Bethlehem Ephrathah, though you are little among the thousands of Judah, yet out of you shall come forth to Me the one to be Ruler in Israel, Whose goings forth are from of old, from everlasting.* (Micah 5:2)

So the "Eternal One" would be born in Bethlehem, and this is declared 700 years before there was a fully-booked inn and a maternity-ward moment in a manger. But here's a bit more. The Bible doesn't simply say Bethlehem; it specifically declares the Messiah to be destined to arrive in "Bethlehem Ephrathah, in Judah." There was more than one Bethlehem in Israel. And Micah predicts the arrival of One whose beginnings and origins would be eternal, and that He would be born here, in "Bethlehem of Judah." How did he know?

We know that Jesus' hometown was Nazareth, which is some 90 miles north of Bethlehem. As Bible students, we've both had the privilege of making that commute, under much easier conditions now in this 21st century! You pass south along the Jordanian border, on to Jericho, and then it's still 20-odd miles to Jerusalem, and another five or six to Bethlehem.

And here's something else. As married men, we know there is no way that a wife in her ninth month of pregnancy would choose to make that 90-mile journey on the back of a donkey. Even in that primitive culture, any caring husband would never request it! So the odds

were small that someone living in Nazareth would leave to
deliver a child over in Bethlehem. If we were interviewing
people on the streets of Nazareth, at the time Mary was six
or seven months pregnant, and were to ask her relatives,
"Where will this Baby be born?" they'd all say: "Right here!
No question. She's not going anywhere." But . . . a decree
of Caesar Augustus brought the holy family, Mary and
Joseph, over those 90 rugged miles to Bethlehem, during
the exact time of Jesus' birth.

How did Micah the prophet know such a thing 700
years before the fact? He never could have, except for the
divine element involved in this entire miraculous story.

We can travel back another eight centuries or so, to the
final moments in the book of Genesis. Moses, of course,
penned the first five books of the Bible, at least 1,500 years
before the birth of Jesus.

In the closing chapters there's a poignant scene where
the dying Jacob is sharing a final testimony and blessing
with his 12 sons. When his fourth son, Judah, stands before
him, the aging patriarch delivers this unique benediction
and prophecy: *"Judah is a lion's whelp; from the prey, my son,
you have gone up. He bows down, he lies down as a lion; and
as a lion, who shall rouse him?"* And then these amazing
words: *"The scepter shall not depart from Judah, nor a lawgiver
from between his feet, until Shiloh comes; and to Him shall be the
obedience of the people."* (Genesis 49:9, 10)

If we were betting Bible students—and were considering
this gamble with its 12-to-1 odds—we probably wouldn't
make such an improbable wager. How could a senile, blind
man on his deathbed possibly know that any son of his, let
alone *which* son, would be the ancestor of the promised
Redeemer? The word "Shiloh" meant *peacemaker*, a title
with divine implications. Everyone in the room, standing
about the deathbed, understood that something special,
something significant was going to happen under Judah's

reign. And Jesus, the Shiloh, the Peacemaker, arrived as a Baby in a manger in the city of Bethlehem, in the province of Judah. Now, with all due respect to our scientific friends who pursue genetic studies with their microscopes and our good teachers who instruct students in matters of biology and sex education, let's thoughtfully look at the prediction found in Isaiah 7:14. Rev. Spong suggests that this is impossible, but God's Word says otherwise. *Therefore the Lord Himself will give you a sign: behold, the virgin shall conceive and bear a Son, and shall call His name Immanuel.*

Seven hundred years before there was even a girl named Mary, these bold words had been written. Some linguists and scholars suggest that the Hebrew word for "virgin," *almah*, simply meant "young woman," and that if Isaiah had meant a sexually pure girl, he would likely have used the more explicit expression, *bethulah*, which clearly means "virgin" and nothing else.

But it's also likely that angels are smarter than we human beings! Hundreds of years later, one of God's winged messengers was trying to explain this very miracle situation to a confused young man named Joseph. He was engaged to his beloved Mary, and was planning to "put her away," and quietly break off the betrothal. He had discovered that Mary was pregnant, and he knew full well this was not something for which he was responsible. Even though it was long before the discovery of the "egg cell", he had a basic knowledge of the facts of life, and knew that this Baby was not his "fact." But he didn't want to embarrass Mary; he still loved and cared for her.

In Matthew, chapter 1, this visiting angel makes it perfectly clear what has happened. *"Joseph, son of David, do not be afraid to take to you Mary your wife, for that which is conceived in her is of the Holy Spirit. And she will bring forth a Son, and you shall call His name Jesus, for He will save His people from their sins."* (v. 20, 21)

Here in Matthew, seven centuries later, the Bible writer clearly links the Isaiah prophecy to this miraculous event, and two verses later uses the clear-cut Greek word, *parthenos*, which also meant "virgin." Mary herself confirms her virginal state to the herald angel in Luke's telling of this same beautiful story.

Now, a question. Isaiah called this miracle a "sign," a prophetic indicator. But if this was simply a case of a "young girl" giving birth to a baby, where is there a sign in that? Young girls had babies all the time; it was as common in ancient Israel as it is today. It would have been a meaningless statement. But sprinkled liberally throughout the inspired writings of the Old Testament we find no fewer than 47 specific prophecies regarding Jesus and the supernatural elements of His birth, life, death, and resurrection; 47 events which indicate that this child, born in Bethlehem, would be the divine Son of God.

Any one of us might take on the role of a supermarket tabloid psychic and, if we were nebulous in our predictions, get one guess right every few years. But 47 times in a row, 47 out of 47, the Bible's inspired writers were accurate in what they wrote about the coming Savior.

How was it then, during those years when Jesus was actually here in our world? Did His disciples believe Him to be the Christ? Did they accept His claims to be something other than just a human being?

As we've already discovered, it was a slow process for them to fully believe. During Jesus' entire ministry, in fact, His friends clung to their previous convictions about a Messiah who would sweep them to temporal power and give them victory over the hated Roman occupiers of their land. Oh, there were flashes of faith as they saw Jesus work miracles and heal the sick, even raising people from the dead; they sometimes caught glimpses of divinity as they sensed the heavenly power of His teaching. Peter, in a rare moment of humble inspiration, blurted out the truth when Jesus asked the twelve: *"Who do men say that I, the Son of Man, am?"* And he replied: *"You are the Christ, the Son of the living God."* (Matt. 16:13,16)

It wasn't really until after Jesus' death and resurrection that the surviving eleven disciples truly believed and began to proclaim that this was the Son of God. They remembered the many times they had seen their Master openly declare a man's sins forgiven. There's a marvelous healing story in Mark 2 where a paralytic man's friends lowered him through a hole in the roof into a crowded home where Jesus was teaching. Scribes and teachers of the law, eager to catch Jesus in a false word, were thrilled when the Man from Nazareth told the broken-down man, *"Son, your sins are forgiven."* And they were absolutely correct when they surmised in their hearts, "We've got Him now! That's blasphemy! Who can forgive sins but God alone?" That's a true statement! Only God *can* forgive sins, but as Jesus was God, it was entirely proper for Him to remove that wretched man's guilt. A moment later He proved He had the divine power to forgive sins, by not only reading their minds, but by healing the man of his physical malady as well.

Of course, standing around the cross on a dark Friday afternoon, the disciples and friends of Jesus saw with their own eyes the predictions of Psalm 22 being fulfilled. They saw His hands and feet pierced with nails. They saw soldiers rolling the dice, casting lots for His castoff robe, just as foretold in this ancient prediction written by King David a full millennium earlier. It's telling, however, to note that in the era of the Israelite kings, there was no such thing as crucifixion! The cross was a cruel practice used by the Romans, adopted, most likely, from the Persians and Carthaginians. It came into vogue in Palestine only during the second century before the birth of Christ.

Historians tell us that the Roman emperor, Constantine, abolished the inhuman practice when he himself became a Christian believer, sometime in the fourth century A.D. Throughout the long history of the Jewish nation, stoning, or sometimes hanging, was always the biblical method of execution. When the Pharisees dragged a woman before Jesus and accused her of committing adultery, the law of Moses called for her sin to be punished by stoning. But here in the words of the Psalmist, we find an uncannily accurate description of the details surrounding the death of Jesus Christ on a cross.

Another evidence of the divine mission of our Lord is found in the Old Testament book of Zechariah, chapter 11. Here we find a cryptic story where the prophet works as a shepherd.

See if this sounds familiar: *Then I said to [the owners], "If it is agreeable to you, give me my wages; and if not, refrain." So they weighed out for my wages thirty pieces of silver. And the Lord said to me, "Throw it to the potter"—that princely price they set on me. So I took the thirty pieces of silver and threw them into the house of the Lord for the potter.* (Zechariah 11:12,13)

Five hundred years later, the Bible writer Matthew tells how Judas Iscariot received thirty pieces of silver for betraying His friend Jesus. Later he was filled with remorse, threw the coins down in front of the priests there in the temple, and went out and hanged himself, a lost man. What did they do with the bribe, the "blood money?" The priests purchased a potter's field, which they used to bury foreigners.

All through the four thousand years of Old Testament history—Moses, Isaiah, Micah, Zechariah—we find these consistent clues and patterns leading us to believe that Jesus Christ came here to fulfill a divine mission. We find objective, quantifiable evidence that an inquiring mind can accept: *born in Bethlehem, born in Judah, born of a virgin, crucified with nails through His hands, sold out for thirty pieces of silver.* The proofs go on and on.

And then, of course, we have the words of Jesus Himself. So many point to Him and say, "I simply look at Jesus as a great teacher, a wise leader." All right, but what did the good Teacher say in His teaching? Did Christ refer to Himself as coming from heaven, of being God's Son?

Even just one Bible passage makes it crystal clear that Jesus declared Himself to be of divine origin. John 8 contains two lengthy discussions between Jesus and His accusers, the scribes and Pharisees. In fact, this comes on the heels of the moment when Jesus prevented the fallen woman caught in adultery from being stoned to death. And Jesus says to them over and over: "My Father sent Me. I witness of Him. I am not of this world. He who sent Me is true. When you lift up the Son of Man, you will know that I am He. I came from God; He sent Me." Finally they had heard enough of what they considered blasphemy, and began to almost shriek at Him: *"Now we know that You have a demon! Abraham is dead, and the prophets; and You say, 'If anyone keeps My word he shall never taste death.' Are You greater than our father Abraham, who is dead? And the prophets are dead. Who do You make Yourself out to be?"* (John 8:52, 53)

That's truly the crux of the matter right there. For two thousand years people have been asking that question. "Jesus, are You what they say? Are You really who *You* claim to be?" In the often sacrilegious yet searching Broadway rock opera, *Jesus Christ Superstar*, that is the signature question in the concluding title song: "Jesus Christ! Jesus Christ! Who are You? What have You sacrificed? Jesus Christ Superstar! Do You think You're who they say You are?" It is a lonely planet's anguished question, and here in John 8 Jesus doesn't hesitate as He replies to the Pharisees: *"Your father Abraham rejoiced to see My day, and he saw it and was glad."* (v. 56)

The Jews, confused and angry, retorted: *"You are not yet fifty years old, and have You seen Abraham?"* (John 8:57) Jesus, with quiet confidence, didn't shade the truth, even though He knew it would hasten the moment of His own crucifixion: *"Most assuredly I say to you, before Abraham was, I AM."* (v. 58)

Before those days of dusty travel around Jerusalem, before the stable and the manger, before the nine months of pregnancy and gossip and rumors, Jesus had existed in heaven's highest courts. He had seen the victories and defeat of King David. He had moved upon the hearts and pens of Isaiah, Micah, and Zechariah. He had created vast worlds in six days. And yes, He had communed often with a faithful servant named Abraham.

But to say such a thing out loud—it would be like one of us holding a press conference and talking about our personal visits with Aristotle or Abe Lincoln. Especially when Jesus used the sacred, holy expression—*I AM*. One Bible commentary describes this as being a claim to divinity "in its absolute sense." There was no "shading" of what Christ was telling His enemies. "I am the self-existent One," He was saying. "I am the One who existed from eternity." We find the parallel Hebrew equivalent to this claim clear back in Exodus 3, where God said to a doubtful Moses: "I AM THAT I AM."

These scholars listening to Jesus were fully aware that He was laying claim to that highest of titles, to be God in the fullest sense. He was claiming to be the One without beginning or end. It's no wonder that in their rage they immediately picked up stones and were ready to kill Him right there.

A declaration of His identity is required again of Jesus as He faced the high priest and the tribunal just before His death. After a number of so-called witnesses and accusers failed to agree on any substantial charge, Caiaphas himself asked Jesus: *"Are You the Christ, the Son of the Blessed?"* (Mark 14:61)

And with the truthfulness of His Father's kingdom on the line, Jesus doesn't hesitate to reply. *"I am. And you will see the Son of Man sitting at the right hand of the Power, and coming with the clouds of heaven."* (v. 62) It's a powerful, explosive scene as the high priest then dramatically rips his sacred robes in two, feigning shock that a mere "human" would take on the prerogatives of divinity.

There are many quiet moments where Jesus, in speaking with His intimate friends, was very plain about His heavenly status. Even as a boy of twelve, the young Jesus already was aware that He had been sent here to do a special work of redemption.

In John 14, when the disciple Philip wistfully wishes they could all know what God the Father is like, Jesus says to him: *"Have I been with you so long, and yet you have not known Me, Philip? He who has seen Me has seen the Father; so how can you say, 'Show us the Father?'"* (John 14:9)

He was claiming full equivalence with the Father who had sent Him. In fact, all through the gospels we find Jesus regularly using—and allowing others to use—divine names to refer to Himself. There are many Bible references where Jesus has the attributes of deity: omnipotence, omniscience, omnipresence, and immutability. Only God (including Jesus) has all power, all knowledge, divine presence throughout the universe, and an unchanging nature of complete love.

The Bible is replete with texts where Jesus fulfills tasks that only a God has a right to do. He creates, forgives sins, judges men and women, has authority over death, claims the right to give immortality. And of course, Jesus willingly accepted the worship of His followers. They often bowed down and worshiped Him; for a mortal man to allow that would be a sin of the highest magnitude.

Paul and Barnabas once had the citizens of Lystra attempt to worship them, and they were zealous and adamant in their stout refusal to tolerate it. *"We too are only men, human like you."* (Acts 14:15) But Jesus was willing to be worshiped because He *was* God.

There is one difficult challenge Bible students face, and that comes in the New Testament book of Colossians, chapter 1. Verse 15 calls Jesus the "image of the invisible God, the *firstborn* over all creation." And some critics have said: "Wait a minute. Firstborn? That must mean Jesus was created, that He had a 'beginning.' Jesus Christ can't be fully God if God the Father 'had' Him at some point." In fact, in the early history of the church, some believers fell into this very error of "Arianism," believing that Jesus had a beginning or that there was a time when He did not exist.

However, we find two very solid answers. First of all, the Word of God uses this word "firstborn" in a number of ways. In the Old Testament, King David is referred to as the "firstborn" son of Jesse, even though the record is clear that David was the youngest of Jesse's sons. However, when he became king, of course, he certainly had the *rank* of being first!

And while the Greek word used here in Colossians can and does sometimes refer to being "firstborn" in the traditional sense—as it does when Jesus is the "firstborn" of Mary—it also can be used to simply describe "first in rank." It's a qualitative word; the firstborn is the one who has the title deed.

The firstborn is not born in the sense of time, but in the sense of quality. Jesus is the firstborn in the sense that He gets all the inheritance of the Father. The firstborn was the one who received the title deed and the one who had the privileges and prerogatives of the Almighty Father. So Jesus has the title deed to heaven; He has the inheritance of eternity. *Firstborn* means that He is the one who has preeminence over all the others. Revelation 1 confirms this honor by describing Jesus as the "the Alpha and Omega, the beginning and the end," echoing the claim of Isaiah 44. Jesus and His Father together encompass all history.

Perhaps, even as you've considered some of these Bible defenses of Jesus as the divine Son of God, you are still wondering. *Couldn't Jesus simply be what much of the world says: a very good man? A great teacher? A political leader who revolutionized a generation with his words of wisdom, and then suffered the tragic death of a misunderstood genius?*

Weigh this obvious reality. If a human being says to his friends, over and over and in many ways: "I am God. I was sent from God. I am here on His mission. I and God the Father are One" . . . one of two things must be reality. Either that man is telling the truth—and He *is* God—or he is a liar and/or lunatic: what one Christian writer famously calls the "I am a poached egg" claim.

Imagine the consternation if we were to go on It Is Written television a week from now and claim to be God. What if we took those thirty minutes and proclaimed to a watching world that Finley or Boonstra were divine, that we could forgive your sins, that we could heal the sick and raise the dead, that we would someday come in the clouds of heaven?

After such a historic broadcasting moment, would you continue to consider us "wise teachers" and "good men?" We can state with some confidence that if either of us did something so evil and foolish, we soon would not be preaching on Christian television. After the men in the white coats came and drove us away, we would instead be preaching to the fence posts on the funny farm. It is simply not possible for someone to be only a "good teacher" and be dishonest or deluded so many times.

Friend, good moral people do not lie. Do you believe Jesus is a lunatic? Do you wonder if He was a fraudulent liar? We hope not! He is the One who can forgive our sins. He is the One who can change our lives. He's everything He ever claimed to be. The evidence is stark and overwhelming that He was resurrected from the dead. Jesus' eleven disciples would never have sacrificed their lives merely for a misguided "good moral teacher"; they would never have been willing to be martyred for what they knew was a lie. The testimony of the Bible is wonderfully clear that Jesus Christ, the Son of God, lives today and is able to forgive us and bless us and love us and save us.

Yes, there really *is* something different about Jesus. In the field of world religious leaders, He stands head and shoulders above the rest. Almost everyone feels the need to acknowledge Him, or at least respond to Him. Maybe that's because the things He said and did demand a response from the human heart.

Nothing draws our attention to Jesus quite like the cross of Calvary. Jesus Himself said in John 12:32: *"And I, if I am lifted up from the earth, will draw all peoples to Myself."*

Have you discovered this for yourself—that there is something irresistible about the cross of Christ? As terrible as it was, there is something about it that demands our attention. Who is this innocent Man who hangs between heaven and earth, asking God to forgive those who did this to Him? Who is this Man whose life was summed up by the simple phrase, "He went about doing good"? Who is this Man who healed the sick, taught with such power that demons fled and crowds would riot; this Man who inspired His followers to bring His message to the whole Roman Empire in a single generation?

Who is this Man, who continues to inspire hearts and change lives almost two thousand years later—the Man Napoleon said millions would die for?

We want to ask you just now, today, as you stand under the Cross of Christ—what do you see? A Roman centurion looked at Him, bowed his head, and reverently said, "Truly this was the Son of God."

Millions more have come to the same conclusion. And the good news is that He is as accessible today as He was on that Friday afternoon. He's waiting, right at this moment, for you to take your first steps in His direction. His nail-scarred hand is reaching out for yours, and the question you're facing is whether or not you will choose to grasp it. Will you claim, right now, all that He is offering You?

PRAYER

Father, thank You so much for sending us Jesus. He's so much more to us than just a good man, more than an ethical philosopher, more than a religious teacher. He's our mighty God and our loving Savior! Today we choose to believe it. We choose to reach out to this Jesus who alone can forgive our sins, who can take away our guilt, who can take away our aching void of emptiness. Jesus, we want Your power in our lives right now, changing us and making us new creations. Thank You for allowing us to flee to Your arms, to love You and be accepted by You. We believe the Bible when it says You will never cast us away, that You are always there for us. In Your saving name we pray, Amen.

CHAPTER *FOUR*

Good God, Bad World...Why?

SHAWN: Some years ago, I met a lady whose husband had been savagely murdered by one of their employees. As a result, she was struggling to make ends meet and keep the family business alive at the same time. It was one of those heart-wrenching scenarios that would drive most people off the deep end.

This woman turned out to be one of the most remarkable individuals I've ever met. With tears streaming down her cheeks, she said to me, "Pastor Shawn, as hard as my life is right now, I want to tell you something. In spite of everything that has happened to me, I'm not angry. I won't pretend that I don't miss my husband, or that times aren't tough without him. But what's really remarkable is how I've been able to forgive the young man who did this. And do you know something? I still love God."

Isn't that an amazing confession? Now, I can honestly tell you that not everyone responds like that. Some people lash out at God with anger and profanity, or even give up on Him altogether. So the question is this—what makes the difference? In a world of incredible suffering, can you still believe in God?

A well-known television personality once poked his finger right into the camera to ridicule the faith of some people who were still clinging to the Lord after a terrible natural disaster had swept through and destroyed their home. As they were desperately packing up to evacuate their house, they hung a sign in the window that said: "Jesus still walks with us."

That was more than the TV host could take. "Get real!" he bellowed. "Listen, God is *not* with you. After all, you're now living in a gymnasium!"

And all around the world, it's likely that many viewers nodded their heads in agreement. Because they too find it hard to believe that a good God can let people suffer. Atheists see the carnage around us—the killer waves, the tornadoes, the "September 11s"—and conclude: "If there is a God, He's either uncaring . . . or impotent and unable to fix this. Either way, what kind of heavenly Father is that?" If God is everything the Bible says He is, if God is love and God is all powerful, and if God is all good, then where in the world did all this evil and suffering come from?

Even those who would like to believe, who look into the shadows of their souls for any flicker of hope, struggle mightily with this question. They wrestle with their doubts. They even wonder, is it possible that God Himself is creating such evil?

Recently in California, it was the sad duty of the state to execute a man named Donald Beardslee. Newspaper reports described how he had shot and killed a 23-year-old girl named Patty; he had also stabbed and choked a 19-year-old, Stacey. Both sordid crimes involved drugs and prostitution, so it was a messy tale. But there was more. Years before committing these crimes, he had spent a number of years in jail for stabbing, choking, and drowning an older woman named Laura. One wonders how an inmate could ever be released from the penitentiary after the first crime enabling him to commit the two later offenses. One law enforcement official observed bleakly: "This guy likes to kill women."

Why? What made him a killer? We don't want to think that any human being could become so evil by himself. What really causes sin and killing and death?

As we read our Bibles, we only have to go through the first 26 verses before we find out that "in the beginning," everything was perfect.

It was a beautiful Friday when the following happened: *Then God said, "Let Us make man in Our image, according to Our likeness; let them have dominion over the fish of the sea, over the birds of the air, and over the cattle, over all the earth and over every creeping thing that creeps on the earth." So God created man in His own image; in the image of God He created him; male and female He created them. (Genesis 1:26, 27)*

Here is the culminating act of Creation Week: the shaping of Adam and Eve. They are made in God's image, so they are perfect. They're flawless. They are holy and untainted. Their very natures are upright and unfallen.

What's more, there's no surrounding sin. As they gaze around them, there aren't any billboards or televisions or unholy images to tempt them. There's only one place where temptation even exists, and as long as they stay away from that "one Tree," all is well. Adam is contented with the reality that there's only one woman around—and she is extremely attractive. So there's no problem there!

Our world's first couple were also blessed with an inward "leaning" or propensity toward righteousness. All of us in this sin-soaked 21st century have a natural inclination in the direction of sin, but this perfect pair did not.

What's more, they had no bad habits. A smoker who has inhaled two packs a day for 30 years is dealing with something much stronger than simple nicotine addiction. Multiple times each day he has gotten that pack out, taken off the cellophane wrapper, handled a cigarette, flicked the lighter, sensed the smoke curling up, savored the accompanying cup of after-dinner coffee that goes with it. After days, and weeks, and months, and years, all of those repeated patterns are a powerful chain of captivity. But Adam and Eve were blessed with a clean slate of no addictions.

However, God had given them one more blessing in addition to that clean slate and pristine garden home. He had also offered them the power of choice. They could obey, or turn away. Love Him or spurn heaven's offer of friendship. They could worship or rebel.

Let's backtrack and explore a question that goes even farther back into the days of mystery that precede the glories of Creation Week. We find that the same scenario of new, holy beings—with freedom of choice—existed in the kingdom of heaven as well.

Too many people get their mental image of the Devil from children's costumes on Halloween, or from cartoons where a lovable imp is wearing a red suit, and has horns, a long tail, and a pitchfork to stoke the fires in the innermost parts of the earth. But is this a true picture of Satan?

The answer is no. The Old Testament book of Ezekiel tells us that Satan (Lucifer) had his beginnings in perfection, just as did our world's first parents. *"You were the anointed cherub who covers; I established you; You were on the holy mountain of God; You walked back and forth in the midst of fiery stones. You were perfect in your ways from the day you were created, Till iniquity was found in you."* (Ezekiel 28:14, 15)

One day in heaven, God created a beautiful, noble angelic being and gave that angel the freedom of choice: because, just as it is down here, if you take away the freedom of choice, you erase the ability to love. Love cannot be forced, cannot be coerced, cannot be programmed. If you take away a being's ability to love, you rob him of the opportunity to be fully happy. God wanted beings who responded to His own love with free choice, not puppets to be manipulated by strings. God didn't sit at a cosmic control center at the nucleus of the universe, undo two screws in the back of Lucifer's head, install a computer chip, and then hit the "on" button to boot him up.

So what happened? For a time—the Bible doesn't tell us how long—all was well. Lucifer was a being of purest light; in fact, his name actually comes from two Latin words: *Lux*, meaning light, and *ferre*, meaning to bear, or to bring. He was the anointed or covering cherub in heaven's highest courts. He stood right next to the throne of God. And he was happy *choosing* to love and worship God.

But all of that slowly changed. Scripture has another revealing passage that draws aside the curtain and permits us to understand this controversy between good and evil. In Isaiah 14:12-14, the mystery of sin is described: *"How you are fallen from heaven, O Lucifer, son of the morning! How you are cut down to the ground, You who weakened the nations! For you have said in your heart: 'I will ascend into heaven, I will exalt my throne above the stars of God; I will also sit on the mount of the congregation on the farthest sides of the north; I will ascend above the heights of the clouds, I will be like the Most High.'"*

You can count those boastful words and see that "I" is mentioned five times! There's no doubt about it—Lucifer's fall was caused by pride. It's possible, as a created being, even as the highest and most honored of all angels, that he was jealous about Jesus' position of authority over him. He began to say what so many of us do: "Why not me?"

In his helpful treatise, *Mere Christianity*, C. S. Lewis notes: "According to Christian teachers, the essential vice, the utmost evil, is Pride. Unchastity, anger, greed, drunkenness, and all that, are mere fleabites in comparison; it was through Pride that the devil became the devil: Pride leads to every other vice: it is the complete anti-God state of mind" (*Mere Christianity*, p. 109).

The tragedy is that this questioning, which grew into full rebellion, didn't happen in a vacuum. Lucifer was a

powerful, charismatic being, and he apparently shared his
discontent with other angels. The New Testament tells us
that open conflict was the tragic result. *And war broke out in
heaven: Michael and his angels fought with the dragon; and the
dragon and his angels fought, but they did not prevail, nor was
a place found for them in heaven any longer. So the great dragon
was cast out, that serpent of old, called the Devil and Satan, who
deceives the whole world; he was cast to the earth, and his angels
were cast out with him.* (Revelation 12:7-9)

It's helpful to Bible students that God's Word plainly
tells us, in Revelation's mysterious passages, that "the
Dragon" is this fallen Lucifer, or Satan. Speaking of this
galactic battle, in Revelation 12:4 we read: *His tail drew a
third of the stars of heaven and threw them to the earth.* Many
interpreters suggest then, that as many as one-third of
heaven's holy angels were deceived by Lucifer's campaign
of whispered lies and joined him in his fateful rebellion.
But we can praise God that two-thirds of the angels in
Paradise remained faithful to their Maker, and that God
had no intention of losing this great controversy. Jesus
Himself, speaking many years before John wrote the
apocalyptic book of Revelation, said to His disciples in
Luke 10:18: *"I saw Satan fall like lightning from heaven."* No,
heaven doesn't lose!

What underlying issues precipitated this "fall" from
deepest space? Why is Satan down here at this very
moment? Again, the key issue was one of Pride. In the
Isaiah passage, where fallen ambition burns so brightly in
the creature they called "Morning Star," he declares to his
admirers: *"I will also sit on the mount of the congregation on the
farthest sides of the north."* Every Jew in Israel knew that the
"mount of congregation" had to be Mount Sinai. It was
north of the camp. It was where God administered His law.
So Lucifer is saying: "I don't want to obey. I want to be the
one who gives the law. I want to be the obey-ee, not the

obeyer." So there is a conflict here over God's throne, a conflict over the law of God.

Pride also leads to Lucifer's unwillingness to worship his Creator. Pride causes him to see his Maker as unfair. He begins to suggest to his friends that God is unjust. Pride blinds him to the obvious truth that God has given him every good thing; he now decides that God must be keeping something back, that God's commands are restrictive. In fact, these are all the suggestions Satan later whispers through his serpentine disguise to Eve at the tree.

All of this makes us think of a question that begs to be asked! Why?! Why would an all-knowing God, who can peer into the future and see the wars and the deaths and the lies and the Holocausts . . . why would God allow Lucifer to take his rebellion into full and deadly bloom? Why not nip it in the bud?

When I was a boy, I grew up with three brothers. Now, we loved our dad and had a good life growing up under his care and protection. But what if I had said to my brothers one day, "You know, actually, I have my doubts about the old man. I'm starting to think he's mean-spirited, that he doesn't want us to have any fun?" And suppose my dad heard about my little diatribe, grabbed me by the arm, took me out back, tied me to a fence post, and shot me full of holes? What if Dad had executed me right there for suggesting that he was a mean guy? There's just the slightest chance my three surviving brothers might have concluded he *was* a mean guy!

Let's extrapolate that fictional story into the glorious corridors of heaven where exists this respected angel, this bearer of light. Earlier in Ezekiel 28, he's described as being the "seal of perfection, full of wisdom and perfect in beauty." Lucifer is clothed with every precious stone; he dwells in the splendor of heaven's own Eden. But now, with all of his magnetic and appealing personality, with all his leadership, he begins to surreptitiously plant the seed of doubt: *God is mean in how He runs His universe. If we cross Him in any way, He'll squash us like bugs.* And if God had chosen that moment in the rebellion timeline to squash Lucifer like a bug and then invite the other angels to attend heaven's first funeral—well more than a third of them might have decided that the late Lucifer did have a valid point.

And what kind of worship would it have been from then on? What kind of singing would the choir have done? All the great anthems about "Fear God in His grandeur" and "Let all the world keep silent before Him" would have taken on a chilling new meaning.

Would it have been better then, as God gazed into the eons of the hidden future, and seeing the horrors of sin, to simply withhold the possibility of falling? Was giving the angels and Adam and Eve the power of choice a cosmic error in judgment? Sometimes sci-fi buffs use the term "Stepford" to describe a society filled just with high-end robots. In the town of Stepford, you see, people are beautiful and they are helpful and they do what they are told. But when a robot wife in Stepford tells her husband, "I love you," her heart really isn't in it, because there isn't any heart to *be* in it.

As fathers, we might kid around and suggest that there were times we might have preferred some antiseptic robot children who would obey us a bit more faithfully. We could go to the computerized control center in the Dad's study, his inner sanctum, and hit a button. And the children would rise like compliant zombies from their beds, pull the sheets straight, fold their clothes, put them away, and then walk stiffly into the kitchen. "Daddy - I - will - eat - my - oatmeal. Daddy - I - will - do - my - homework."

That doesn't sound so bad, but at the end of the day,

when the fire is burning warmly in the fireplace, and you've downloaded a new bedtime story onto your kids' factory-installed hard drives, would it bring comfort and joy to your soul to have your iron children put their iron-cold hands up by your face and recite in digital unison: "Daddy - I - love - you - love - you - love - you"?

I know that there's nothing like my little girls, Natalie and Naomi, coming over and climbing up in my lap. They have sleep in their eyes, their noses running a bit. They put their arms around me, the squeaky-clean smell of shampoo still in their hair. "Daddy, I love you," they say, their damp hair getting my shirt collar wet as they nuzzle up close to me. And I know they mean it. It's not from a computerized (.wav) file; this is love springing from their hearts. We want love to be spontaneous, not forced, not demanded at gunpoint.

And God is the same way. Unless we had the freedom to choose against God, what does our choice to follow Him mean? It's like the army private who looks into his locker and then decides: "I think I'll wear my green shirt today." What else is there but green shirts?

With the freedom to sin, with the possibility of sin, has now come the sorry reality of sin. We are all sinners. Our first parents followed Lucifer into rebellion, and we followed right behind them. And along with the sin came the sorrow and the cemeteries.

Here in California, where people have their faults and the geography does too, our homeowner insurance policies sometimes inform us that we are covered except for one thing. What is it? "Acts of God." If God creates a disaster—this is the impression they give us—then the good hands of the insurance companies will no longer hold us up and care for us. But where do calamities come from? If there is a Devil and there is a God, then why do they call the hurricanes acts of God?

As we entered a new year in 2005, we were gripped with horror as on our TV sets we witnessed, in quick succession, a devastating tsunami, a killer mudslide that swallowed up homes and ten precious people, and then a Metrolink train crash caused by a suicidal man parking his SUV on the train tracks. Did God do those things? Did God reach down and make the tectonic plates shift deep in the ocean, displacing trillions of tons of water and stirring up a 500-miles-per-hour wave that would ravage coastlines, destroy homes, and kill nearly 300,000 people? Is this how God operates? Is this how He punishes evil?

It's true that the Lord of all heaven and earth has the power both to start and to stop storms. Jesus revealed that mighty authority while He was here on earth. The book of Exodus does have God sending ten clearly labeled plagues of warning to a rebellious Pharaoh in Egypt. But God does not use a surging sea of water to take the lives of innocent people. Today's natural disasters are the stark result of a world that has separated itself from God. When our world moves away from God, then human beings are affected. Nature itself is affected. A planet that is spinning in rebellion, wearing out, is going to have its tectonic plates shift. The hurricanes are going to blow. Wildfires are going to leap across freeways and parking lots. But these are not conscious, deliberate acts of an angry God. No, they are the natural results of a fallen world that is "wearing old" like a garment; Romans 8 describes this tired planet as "groaning for deliverance." And it is Satan, who has led his captives into this separatist movement, who delights in seeing people swept to premature deaths when the tidal waves reach shore.

True, there are disasters all around. And Satan, the great accuser, has been hurling his charges against God for a long time. "Acts of God." "He doesn't care." "Unfair." "Withholding happiness." "God's law is tyrannical." Etc.

But in the Old Testament book of Job, we see a powerfully revealing story of human faith . . . as well as a portrayal of the behind-the-scenes drama between good and evil.

Here the Bible talks about a council meeting in heaven; Satan, as the rebel leader of this one lost world, comes right up to the heavenly gates and demands to participate. As the rulers of the many unfallen worlds in God's sin-free universe gather around the great council table, Lucifer is there among them. And he taunts his Maker. He gives the God he used to worship an "in-your-face" challenge. "Look at Your servant, Job," he sneers. "Of course he worships You. You've given him everything. You've bought his affections with full barns and ten beautiful children. You've given him rain for his crops and sunshine for his picnics. You've treated him so well he's one step away from being a 'Stepford' servant of Yours. The only worship You're ever going to get from people on my planet is robot worship."

Then the challenge: "Just withdraw Your hand, God. Just take away the hedge of protection. Let me do what I do best for a little while, and then we'll see if Job still serves You and sings Your praises."

And so there came marauding bands of invading armies, lightning bolts from the skies, terrorist raiding parties, and hurricanes. They only hit one ranch—Job's. Before he could blink, his herds were gone, his servants, his children, his everything. The only two things that weren't gone were the boils Satan inflicted in Round Two, and Job's wife. It's a toss-up as to which of those two caused him more misery. (See story in Job 1:6-2:10)

Where did the hurts come from? The Bible says with emphatic clarity that Satan brought every one of them. *"All that he has is in YOUR power,"* God tells His archenemy. Amazingly, through it all, Job doesn't curse God.

The story of Job is the story of faithfulness in trial. It's the story of a man who refused to curse God and to deny God and to shake his fist in God's face even though he's being tried. In fact, it's right here in this drama, when things could not possibly get worse, that Job declares with unparalleled courage: *"Though He slay me, yet will I trust Him."* (Job 13:15) And when we read through the give-and-take of this cosmic drama and get to the last pages of Job, this faithful servant says to his Creator: *"I know that You can do everything. And that no purpose of Yours can be withheld from You."* (Job 42:2)

At the conclusion, God, who has watched the unfolding of these great events, gives His friend back all that had been taken by the enemy. *Now the Lord blessed the latter days of Job more than his beginning; for he had fourteen thousand sheep, six thousand camels, one thousand yoke of oxen, and one thousand female donkeys. He also had seven sons and three daughters.* (Job 42:12, 13) At the end of Job's life, he again had satisfaction, happiness and joy.

Did Job suffer? Yes! Was he faithful in that suffering? Yes. But he came through the suffering and pain better off than before, more blessed than he could have dreamed. And in our world of tsunamis, mud slides, divorces and trials, it may be hard to echo the words of this Old Testament hero of faith: *"Though He slay me, yet will I trust Him."* But if we do hang on in faith, and refuse to let go of our trust, watch what happens! God will stay close by our side as well, and bless us dramatically.

What an honor to be among those who help God answer the lies of Lucifer here in this world! We can be among those who say: "No! God *is* fair! I've found that His kingdom does bring me happiness, even when hard things happen. Instead of holding things back, I find that He has filled my life with blessings."

In his book, *Who You Are (When No One's Looking)*, Bill Hybels writes: "Jesus is the exact opposite of a thief. He does not come to rob but to give. He does not break into anyone's life; He stands at the door and knocks. If invited in, He wanders around the house placing precious objects on the mantels, on the shelves and in the cupboards. He fills up the person's life with everything life is worth living for: purpose, fulfillment, meaning, love, peace, confidence, security, and even freedom." (*Who You Are When No One's Looking*, p. 104)

One challenge that the Job of today may face is this: while the hurricane blows his house over, his unrepentant next-door neighbor continues to live in sunshiny splendor. In Psalm 73, one of King David's great choir leaders, Asaph, complains about this answered-prayer-in-reverse syndrome, where the locusts—rather than skipping over the believer's house—attack *only* his house!

Meanwhile, drunkards and nearby Mafia chiefs ride around in limousines and enjoy their girlfriends and caviar. *"I was envious of the boastful,"* this confused musician confesses, *"when I saw the prosperity of the wicked. For there are no pangs in their death. But their strength is firm. They are not in trouble as other men. Therefore pride serves as their necklace; Violence covers them like a garment."* (Psalm 73:3-6)

Once again, Satan's accusation that God is unfair seems to gain some ground here. But is it possible that God sometimes allows wicked people to prosper so they can see that their blessings come from Him and then turn to Him even in their prosperity? Can God's faithful servants stand on the sidelines and patiently wait while God gives abundance and blessings to other people, hoping to woo them with His generosity?

And if perchance the sunshine fails to melt a rebel's heart, is it possible that God might reluctantly do as the old song says—"Into every life some rain must fall?" Yes, that could happen. Maybe the wicked person who seems to be prosperous today, if he doesn't turn to God, with the gentle overtures of His love and prosperity, could lose a son or daughter to cancer. Not caused by God, but allowed by Him. Maybe a divorce happens and a marriage breaks up. Again, not caused by God but allowed as the natural result of their own choices. And perhaps that unsaved, rebellious person, who seems so on top of the world today, is so crushed and bruised tomorrow that he will make the right decision and turn to God.

On the other hand, God may allow tragedies to come into our lives too . . . as a way of calling us to deepen our Christian experiences. We're encouraged in Hebrews 12: 11 by this: *Now no chastening seems to be joyful for the present, but grievous; nevertheless, afterward it yields the peaceable fruit of righteousness to those who have been trained by it.*

When I was a boy, I had to have surgery done on both of my legs. It was exceptionally painful. But once the pain subsided, it enabled me to walk and to have a normal life. Even though disease and physical afflictions are an invention of the Devil, God permitted me to go through that time and I became stronger as a result.

During our hard times, we are sometimes tempted to wonder if God is simply "sitting on the sidelines," not caring about our pain. It must be pretty easy for Him, we think darkly, and here we are bearing such a heavy load. Why doesn't He help us? How much longer must we wait?

MARK: A number of years ago, while traveling through Europe, I visited the dreaded concentration camp, Dachau. It represented the worst of what Nazi Germany had done to innocent people. Talk about a work inspired by Satan! I walked with a heavy heart through the very area where the ovens and crematoriums were. And to sense that people were gassed in those chambers, and put in those ovens and burned, with the smoke going up day after day into the air of totalitarian fear—it was a somber moment for me. I was meditating and near tears as I witnessed the ghosts of this evil regime. I too had this thought: "God, where were You? How could You permit these atrocities? Where in the world were You when Dachau was happening?"

Then I walked into a cell, and etched into the wall by some lonely, anonymous prisoner were these words: "God was here."

This is the good news even today. A tsunami slams into an unsuspecting city on the day after Christmas—and God is there in the hands of the volunteers who come to help. God is present in the generosity of those who go online and make a sacrificial gift that means they will do without some holiday comfort. God is there in the healing touch of doctors who cancel their own vacation, jump on a plane, and fly to Phuket or Banda Aceh to help.

Yes, every time there is sorrow, God is there. And often the difference between the saved and the unsaved person—as both feel the dark waters swirling up to their waists—is that while both may suffer, the saved person has an absolute confidence. He's made a conscious choice to have God by his side; he's chosen to believe that God hasn't left him in his suffering. He may feel alone, but he has chosen to cling to the knowledge that he is not alone. That in suffering, God is where He always is: *present.*

That is where God was when His own Son died. On the cross, Jesus couldn't feel His presence, He couldn't sense it, but He continued to cling to the knowledge of it. Even as spiritual darkness suggested that His Father had forsaken Him, as He *felt* alone in His suffering, Jesus was able to commit His spirit to the Father who was still present.

You remember the classic Mary Stevenson essay about the person who looks back over his life and is thankful for the two sets of footprints along the beach. We could expand the story and observe that in some of our dark valleys, yes, there were the two sets of prints, as God walked along side as a Protector. In the mountains of great challenge, the two sets of prints again revealed a God who guides us on the treacherous trails.

But then in one particularly deep chasm, a time of deepest discouragement, we see just one set of footprints. Why, God? Why, when I needed You most, does it look like You were absent? My life was crushed and broken. I was desperate for Your presence, and it looks like I had to go through that time of travail without You. In Stevenson's poignant words, "Why, when I have needed You most, You have not been there for me."

And the Lord gently tells us to look at that one set of prints more closely. The prints are deeper than usual (and not even your size!). Why? It was then that the Lord picked us up and carried us in His mighty arms. Often without knowing it, we were resting on His shoulders.

In those moments, we can join King David and his friend Asaph in looking to the future. Shawn and I have traveled around the world and seen this planet's deepest scars. We've seen people dying in hospitals with terminal cancer, and men and women surviving in the former Soviet Union whose husbands or wives were killed by the oppressive communist regime.

We've seen people who went to the gulags or prisons because of their religious beliefs and emaciated survivors in Rwanda who saw their loved ones hacked into pieces in that country's genocide.

Yet, through it all, the Christians who have endured these horrors have kept an optimistic, even buoyant spirit. Why? Because they believe that there's a new heaven and a new earth! They believe that Jesus will come again! They believe that . . . *the Lord Himself will descend from heaven with a shout, with the voice of an archangel, and with the trumpet of God. And the dead in Christ will rise first. Then we who are alive and remain shall be caught up together with them in the clouds to meet the Lord in the air. And thus we shall always be with the Lord.* (I Thessalonians 4:16, 17)

Yes, Christians have been "comforting one another" with those words for a long time. Praise God! The great hope of this world is that Jesus Christ is coming. And soon all of the sorrow, all of the suffering, all of the death will be over.

What will it be like then? Today, because of this great war, we are in enemy-occupied territory where the war is still going on. God's victory is assured because of Calvary, but the bullets are still hitting their mark. And our loving Father, because of the rebellion, has had to do some letting go. This is why the tectonic plates shift and the tidal waves rise up in their wrath. This is sin at its desperate worst.

But picture the day when this tired old planet is made well, healed, restored. Somehow in the glorious centuries that follow, we will still be on this world, but now held fast in God's loving hand. The tectonic plates will be secure, safe, stitched together by His healing power. No more earthquakes; no more mudslides; no more lost homes and broken hearts.

Here is another mystery. You and I, as God's redeemed trophies, will still be men and women with the power of choice! We will be holy beings, still free and able to choose and think and love. In fact, we will be freer then than we are today, because right now we are victims of so many fallen habits and addictions. In God's earth made new, we will stand tall with liberty from all those besetting sins and harmful patterns.

But how can we know, in that perfect world—as freedom continues—that we might not fall again? True, Lucifer will be gone. His army of demons will have been erased from the universe. Temptations and the stimuli of sin will have been banished. We will be surrounded by holy friends and guardian angels. And we have God's sure word of promise found in Nahum 1:9: *What do you conspire against the Lord? He will make an utter end of it. Affliction will not rise up a second time.*

Is it possible that, just as God will hold this reborn planet in His hands and keep the world safe and the storms away, that He will also hold His redeemed children in His hands and keep us pure forever *while* allowing us to still retain the full liberty that leads to purest love? He has always longed for just such a family—sons and daughters who no longer desire sin—a kingdom that has been through this Great Controversy, this long war, and now comes through on the other side to live in full liberty forever.

Aren't the richest marriages the ones where a husband and wife are both free, yet locked together *by love?* Aren't the happiest families bound together by that common bond of loyalty and friendship?

Aren't the best churches, the most vibrant fellowships, the ones with no traces of a rigid "cult" hierarchy? Where the members aren't there because of mind control, or a charismatic leader who binds their consciences with his overbearing personality. Where there are no locks on the doors or people aren't required to stay. But they *do* stay because love has captured their hearts. They would rather worship Jesus than do anything else in all the world. They enjoy a spiritual liberty that is safeguarded *by love.*

There are no robots among these fortunate ranks; anyone could leave at any time . . . but they don't. Why? Their hearts are knit together for eternity *by love.*

What will it be like to live forever in that land of peace and happiness? To be held fast by God's strong, gentle hands? To freely *choose* each day to be His child?

This is the New World, the better land that God envisions and offers us.

Here's how the Bible anticipates it: *For I consider that the sufferings of this present time are not worthy to be compared with the glory which shall be revealed in us. For the earnest expectation of the creation eagerly waits for the revealing of the sons of God. For the creation was subjected to futility, not willingly, but because of Him who subjected it in hope; because the creation itself also will be delivered from the bondage of corruption into the glorious liberty of the children of God.* (Romans 8:18-21)

Of course, that will be *then*. This is *now*. And Bible quotes about a peaceful Paradise in the distant future don't put a roof over your head today or food in your hungry child's stomach tonight.

But *now* is when we have Jesus! He is your Friend, your ever-present help even as you read these words. In the very center of God's plan to secure the eternal happiness of the universe . . . we find the cross of Jesus. It's a startling and daily reminder that God has not chosen to distance Himself from our troubles.

Speaking about the Messiah hundreds of years in advance, the prophet Isaiah wrote: *He is despised and rejected by men, A Man of sorrows and acquainted with grief* (Isaiah 53: 3) As a sympathetic Savior who was our "Man of sorrows," there is no suffering Jesus doesn't understand.

Do you suffer with loneliness, cut off from your loved ones? Jesus' own family mocked and misunderstood Him.

Do you lay awake at night with anguish of the mind? So did Jesus. That last Thursday night in the Garden of Gethsemane, Jesus wrestled against the weight of our sins to the point where, in agony, the blood began to ooze through His skin.

Do you suffer from a sense of hopelessness and abandonment? Remember that anguished cry from Calvary: *My God, My God, why have You forsaken Me?*

In Jesus, God Himself experienced every facet of our human suffering. He didn't disappear to some distant, safe corner of the universe when the trouble started. He didn't exclude Himself from our hurts. No, He stood at the grave of His friend and wept. He endured unbelievable physical agony and suffered mental anguish. He knew firsthand the pain of rejection.

So whatever it is today that you are enduring in pain, He knows all about it.

Maybe you've been carrying your struggles all by yourself, and it's getting just a little hard to bear. The Bible promises that you can take your problems—your heartache, your disappointment—and bring them right to heaven's sanctuary. There you'll find a God who carries scars of His own, because He wants you so desperately in His kingdom. Is it your greatest desire to be with Him?

PRAYER

Father, someone reading these words is hurting just now. Maybe a woman whose husband has died of cancer, or in an accident, leaving her children fatherless. Perhaps someone has lost a son or daughter in the horrors of an overseas war. Someone may now be sick in bed with a terminal disease. Someone may be languishing in a prison cell, knowing in their heart they have been unjustly accused and condemned. We pray for these precious children of Yours just now, Lord. We live in a world of unfairness, but help us through our tears and our pain and our suffering to see Jesus, standing by our side with His arms around us to give us hope and courage. We thank You so much that You are there in the midst of our trials. And we thank You that we can turn to You in every emergency with the confidence that You will never let us down. In Christ's saving name, Amen.

CHAPTER FIVE

The Path to the Top

Christian writer John Stott tells the story about a social worker living in Nigeria who dropped by to see a young man who lived in the slums of Lagos. Evidently this youth was searching for truth, because on the little nightstand next to his bed were the following: the Bible, the Anglican *Book of Common Prayer*, a copy of the Koran, three copies of a magazine called *Watchtower*, describing the philosophy of the Jehovah's Witnesses, a biography of Karl Marx, and even a book of yoga instructions! Oh, and one thing more: a popular paperback with this title: *How to Stop Worrying*. Pastor Stott observes wryly that he probably needed that book the most! ("The Uniqueness of Jesus Christ," *The Contemporary Christian*, p. 296)

Mountaineers have proven that there are several acceptable ways to scale the world's highest mountain and get yourself up to the peak of Everest. It's said that "all roads lead to Rome." And of course, while you say toe-*may*-toe, others may prefer to say toe-*mah*-toe. Does it matter? Doesn't it all taste the same anyway? Some people, like that young seeker in Nigeria, finally suggest that there's just no such thing as a "wrong" approach to religion. "It's all a matter of personal taste," they conclude. "The most important thing is that you find your own way to express your spirituality."

Yet those who stop to seriously consider this claim soon run into a little bit of trouble. Common sense tells us that everybody can't be right at the same time, especially when they disagree. We've all had the experience of having a math teacher hand back to us the test we took last week and the many red marks all over the paper point out that sometimes our answers are wrong. We all know there are many instances in life where there is only one right answer.

We should say this kindly, but when you examine the teachings and behavior of some of the religious "nut cases" running around in our world, you know in your heart that everybody can't be right.

Consider, for example, Brian David Mitchell, the man who abducted young Elizabeth Smart and held her as a spiritual slave for long months. He was a religious man, wasn't he?

Then there are the cases of Charles Manson, David Koresh, Jim Jones and Dr. Luc Jouret's Solar Temple, in which 53 cult members committed suicide. In every one of those tragic stories, nobody would dare to suggest that those religions weren't flat-out wrong and fatally flawed.

When it comes down to mainstream religion, modern thinking has suggested that it's inappropriate to apply any sort of value judgment to them. "Leave well enough alone," the postmodern man says. "There's proof of some validity in every religion. Let's include Mohammed and Jesus and Confucius and Buddha and everybody."

This same Dr. Stott quotes from Dr. W. A. Visser't Hooft, who served as the first General Secretary of the World Council of Churches, and who actively worked with fellow Christian John Weidner during World War II to help Jewish refugees and Allied airmen escape from the Nazis.

In his book, *No Other Name*, he defines syncretism as the view "that there is no unique revelation in history, that there are many different ways to reach the divine reality, that all formulations of religious truth or experience are by their very nature inadequate expressions of that truth, and that it is necessary to harmonize as much as possible all religious ideas and experiences so as to create one universal religion for mankind." (*No Other Name*, p. 11)

Does he subscribe to this view himself? Absolutely not! Dr. Visser't Hooft immediately goes on to declare: "It is high time that Christians should rediscover that the very heart of their faith is that Jesus Christ did not come to make a contribution to the religious storehouse of mankind, but that *in Him God reconciled the world unto Himself.*" In other words, as theologians put it, the Christian gospel is *sui generis*—unique.

Does Christianity itself claim to be exclusive? Does it proclaim itself as the only path to heaven?

We must answer that question wisely and carefully, because on the one hand Christianity is the most *inclusive* faith the world has ever seen! The claim of Christianity is that the entire world must hear and know Jesus Christ. The passion-filled Gospel Commission, found in Matthew 28: 19, 20, says: *"Go therefore and make disciples of ALL the nations, baptizing them in the name of the Father and of the Son and of the Holy Spirit, teaching them to observe all things that I have commanded you; and lo, I am with you always, even to the end of the age."* Amen.

Our Lord clearly told us to take the gospel of Jesus everywhere in a most inclusive way! We both have held Christian evangelistic meetings in the great cities of the world. On our billboards and handbills the invitation has always read—in the common language of those people groups—"Everyone Invited!" Every time we have set up a web site in a foreign land, we've never put up "blockers" to keep out certain undesired groups. We've never posted sentinels at the stadium entrances to screen out who might come in to hear the invitation of Jesus.

In Revelation 14, where we find the glorious proclamations of the three angels flying in the skies above, the first proclamation states: *Then I saw another angel flying in the midst of heaven, having the everlasting gospel to preach to those who dwell on the earth—to every nation, tribe, tongue, and people."* (Revelation 14: 6) So this is a message of inclusion.

What's more, the student of God's Word soon finds that in genuine, pure Christianity, there is no racism, no classism, no caste system, no gender exclusiveness. In genuine Christianity, in coming to Jesus Christ, men and women are bonded together in a common salvation that makes them equal. It's an equality, based not on education, or wealth, or eucharistic or ethnic background—it's an equality in Jesus Christ! In Galatians 3:28, Paul writes to the infant Christian church: *There is neither Jew nor Greek, there is neither slave nor free, there is neither male nor female, for you are all one in Christ Jesus.*

Our Christian ethic teaches that we are all created by God; in this, God gives us a bondedness.

We also have the ringing declaration by Jesus Himself, declaring: *"And I, if I am lifted up from the earth, will draw all peoples to Myself."* (John 12:32)

In terms of the desire of heaven, Christianity is absolutely *inclusive.* As far as God is concerned, He has expressed His will once for all time in II Peter 3:9: *[He] is longsuffering toward us, not willing that any should perish but that all should come to repentance.* His last-day invitation to Planet Earth reads like this: *And the Spirit and the bride say, "Come!" And let him who hears say, "Come!" And let him who thirsts come. Whoever desires, let him take the water of life freely.* (Revelation 22:17)

But the Christian faith is also *exclusive*. Honest research and Bible study forces us to conclude so. In the book of Acts, we don't find that there are many pathways to heaven, or an abundance of trails that lead us to the mountaintop. After writing about the Cornerstone—the crucified and risen Jesus—which the builders rejected, Luke writes these words under the direction of the Holy Spirit: *Nor is there salvation in any other, for there is no other name under heaven given among men by which we must be saved.* (Acts 4:12)

Notice: there is just one name that brings salvation. No book on your nightstand can save. No magazine can save. And the Word of God is abundantly clear as well that we cannot be saved by the teachings or the lives of Buddha, Mohammed, and Confucius.

Now why? Millions of devout people throughout the world are adherents of the monk who wore a saffron robe and taught his followers to deny self, to be kind to others, to seek inner peace. Why is there no salvation, then, to be found in the Buddhist faith?

That takes us to a more basic question: what is salvation? We all would agree—and the Bible plainly teaches—that salvation must involve forgiveness of sins. It entails the power of a living God to change our lives. Salvation includes a gift by the Author of eternal life, giving us the hope of life beyond the grave.

Can Buddha offer us forgiveness, or Confucius, or Mohammed? No. Only the One we have sinned against can offer us such forgiveness. So if Jesus Christ is indeed the divine Son of God, and we've sinned *against God*, only Christ can legitimately offer us forgiveness of sin. Buddha may offer enlightenment; Confucius may offer wisdom; Mohammed may offer a way of life to his followers . . . but can they provide the resurrection power from the dead? Did they, themselves, emerge from the tomb in victory? Buddha is said to have feebly whispered to his devotees before expiring: "Strive without ceasing." Popular Hinduism can suggest nothing more hopeful than the idea of trying a bit harder, doing a bit more, growing a bit more spiritual in a never-ending series of lives where one tries to eventually defeat bad karma. John Stott concludes: "From this endless cycle (samsara) of rebirths or reincarnations there is no escape by forgiveness." ("The Uniqueness of Jesus Christ" *The Contemporary Christian*, p. 311)

In the religion of Islam, mercy is offered to people who, in a bit of an oxymoron, "earn" it by meritorious good deeds, by those who pray and give alms and fast during the feast of Ramadan. But is there forgiveness, a way for sinners to escape from judgment? No.

Jesus Himself, in loving kindness, and as a gracious warning, tells us plainly that there is one exclusive way back to the Father. We might eavesdrop on a midnight conversation He had with a sincere seeker of truth named Nicodemus. As Jesus is talking with Nicodemus we hear Him use both the *exclusive* AND *inclusive* in John 3:16, the most beloved verse in the Bible. This text is treasured in cultures around the world, as it plainly says: *"For God so loved the world that He gave His only begotten Son, that whoever believes in Him should not perish but have everlasting life."*

The very next verse declares that God is willing to save "the world" through His Son Jesus. Christ Himself declares that He is the way, that He is the Door, that He is the gate, the pathway, the vine, the bread and water of life, the "way and the truth and the life." (John 14:6) He repeatedly linked salvation with a belief in Him. But a modern-day seeker might ask, "What specifically does Jesus do for me? How am I saved?"

In earlier chapters, we've explored the realities of this fallen world. Sin is all around us. It's our nature to be sinners. When Adam and Eve, using their free will and power of choice, decided to disobey, the entire human

race was plunged into a rebellion against God. Isaiah 59:
2 tells us: *But your iniquities have separated you from your God;
and your sins have hidden His face from you, so that He will not
hear.* While still at that forbidden tree in Eden, Adam and
Eve began to experience the cold chill of separation from
God, separation from the source of life, separation from
the source of love, the source of their peace and joy.

And of course, to be separate from the source of life
is to eventually die! There are two cosmic powers in our
universe: love and hate. Hate really is the "last straw." Hate
leads to separation from God. While love always leads a
person to the building up of life and joy and happiness,
hate and selfishness destroys to the core.

While standing at the tree of deception, Adam and Eve
became separated from the source of life and love. They
now had the seeds of death in their bodies; there was no
possibility that they could live forever. The Bible warns in
Romans 6:23: *"The wages* [that is, the natural result of the
consequence of a life independent, separated from God]
of sin is death. And doesn't this make sense? If God is the
generous Creator and Sustainer of all things, and we cut
ourselves off from that very Source of all life, what do we
have? It's like a branch that has been cut off the apple tree.
It immediately begins to die.

So we were created to live forever. But that gift of
immortality was conditional . . . upon our ongoing relationship with God.

When the human race fell from grace and severed itself
from Life, what was God in heaven to do? Could the Father
and the Son and the Spirit have simply pushed earth out
into deeper space and isolated it behind a "Berlin Wall"
for badness? Quarantined the rebellion for all eternity?
Could they have allowed Adam's descendants to spiral into
an endless cycle of murder and self-extinction? Thankfully,
God refused to do these things!

We can also be thankful that the emergence of sin in God's universe was not an unexpected crisis for the Father. In His divine foreknowledge, He knew of the possibility of a rebellion. It says in I Peter 1:20 that Jesus was foreordained "before the foundation of the world" to be the Lamb that would be sacrificed. Jesus was willing to come to Bethlehem; He stepped forward and said: "Father, I will live the perfect life that Mark Finley should have lived. I will obey perfectly the way that Shawn Boonstra failed to; I will live on earth and be completely submissive to Your holy will, the way John and Jane Doe weren't able to. I will live the life they should have lived; I will walk over the same territory; I will face the same temptations of all humanity." (See Hebrews 4:15)

This is good news, because it means our Savior is near to us. He's like us. He took on human flesh. He experienced all of the struggles and sinful invitations of human flesh. He defeated Satan in the flesh. And then He went to the cross and He died the death that all of us deserve. Hebrews 2:9 encourages us with the news that *He, by the grace of God, might taste death for everyone.* (Talk about *inclusive!*)

Only the Christian faith, only the wonderful Person of Jesus Christ, offers this unique and life-saving gift. II Corinthians 5:21: *For He [God] made Him [His Son] who knew no sin to be sin FOR us, that we might become the righteousness of God in Him.* Again we see that this offer is generously inclusive . . . but provided through the exclusive one-of-a-kind gift of God's only Son. We have the privilege today of coming to Jesus and saying, "Lord, I accept that death in my behalf. You have already provided for my salvation on the cross, and by faith I accept it."

But now we come face to face with the very difficult issue of the *exclusive* part of the contract. We have both heard this hard question posed many, many times as we've shared the gospel. "If Jesus Christ is the only way to heaven, then what about that native living in a remote tribe somewhere on an island out in the Pacific who never heard about Him? Where is the fairness of God in excluding him? He never laid eyes on a Bible; no missionaries ever visited him; his simple hut never housed a television on which to watch It Is Written. He never had an opportunity to hear the truth. So what about him?"

The gospel is like a two-sided coin. The one side of the coin is crystal clear: *there is no salvation outside of Jesus Christ.* He is the only method of salvation; there is no other. Buddhism is not a method of salvation. Confucianism is not a method of salvation. Mohammed does not provide a method of salvation. But we read in Romans chapter 1 that salvation can only come through the Christian gospel—*for the Jew first and also for the Greek.* In chapter two, we read about tribulation and anguish for those who are sinning outside of a relationship with Jesus—*the Jew first and also of the Greek.* In Romans 3 it's the same: *All have sinned and fall short of the glory of God.* But then in chapters 4-6, the good news is that God credits righteousness to those who believe in Jesus. We have "peace with God" through Jesus. We are accounted "dead to sin and alive with Christ."

So one side of the coin is that we are all lost without Jesus. The flip side, the good news side, is that a gracious, merciful, loving God knows the background of every single human being. It's not that they are saved through the philosophical system, or the religious system they are in—but it is possible to be saved in God's kingdom by a Christ they do not yet know and have not yet come to comprehend. In *Mere Christianity,* C. S. Lewis conjectures: "We do know that no man can be saved except through Christ; we do not know that only those who know Him can be saved through Him." (p. 65)

A number of years ago, our It Is Written ministry was surprised when a plain brown package came in the mail one day. There was no return address, no indication of its origin. Nobody signed their name to it. UPS had no details we could glean. But inside that bare, nondescript envelope were *seventy* $100 bills! In a rare moment of anonymous goodness, a loving friend had decided to send us $7,000 to help proclaim God's message of salvation.

We did not know the source of that windfall. We had no way to thank the giver for his or her generosity. *But we did use the money with tears of rejoicing!* We experienced the bounty of that love gift . . . and someday, perhaps in heaven, when God or a faithful saint finally whispers their identity to us, we will be able to say: "It was you! Thank you! We were so grateful for the gift, and now are honored to take your hand and express our love and appreciation."

Borrowing just one more line from John Stott's book, he describes the Christian perspective of *Inclusivism* this way: It "allows that salvation is possible to adherents of other faiths, but attributes it to the secret and often unrecognized work of Christ." (*The Contemporary Christian*, p. 297)

Think of a faithful Buddhist, living and eking out a spartan existence in one of the fishing villages of southern Thailand. He makes just a few *baht* a day catching fish and selling them in the local market. He feeds his three children and is kind to his wife, all as dictated by the only faith he has ever known. He sees the beautiful sunsets off Phuket Island; he marvels that God has made such a world. When God whispers in his ear, through his conscience, to be honest with others, to be kind to his neighbors, to be faithful in his marriage, he responds and lives a life loyal to his conscience.

Then, on December 26, 2004, a tsunami hits that village, and sends this man to a watery grave. He never once saw a Bible. The three channels he got on his little television set didn't have Christian programs. No missionaries made it down from Bangkok to his small town to share the good news about Calvary. And yet, is it possible that God in His loving wisdom was able to draw out a response from that man's honest heart?

There's a tender word of hope that we find in the 87th chapter of Psalms. True, there are those who are fortunate to be born in places where the good news of the gospel is found up on billboards. But what of the others? What will God do about them?

It says in verse 6: *The Lord will record when He registers the peoples, "This one was born there."* This verse is beautifully amplified in *The Clear Word*, which is a personal paraphrase: "Yes, the Lord records all who are His and will take into consideration where a man was born and where he grew up." (Jack Blanco, *The Clear Word*, p. 689)

Yes, we have an infinite God who is motivated to weigh the hard circumstances of every life, who knows the opportunities and pitfalls each of us face. Salvation is not a geographical lottery game! Both of us were privileged to grow up in the heartland of Christian nations, where churches dotted the landscape and where Bibles could be purchased for a dollar. Christianity was in the heritage we inherited. But God is equally determined to reap a harvest in lands where the good news of the gospel was perhaps heard but faintly.

Is there salvation outside of Christ? No. But who is saved and not saved is a question we must leave in the hands of our merciful Jesus. It certainly is not our role to play God and muse about the fates of others. Jesus knows their background; He knows what their understanding is; He also knows what it *could have been*. It may well be that some will find themselves in God's kingdom, wide-eyed and beside themselves with joy, who don't understand where the gift of salvation has come from. They have never heard the name of Jesus . . . but they will hear it there from

His own lips! That decision is up to God and we should humbly let God *be* God.

There's a precious little verse found in the brief, one-chapter book of Jude, just before the thunder and the smoke of Revelation. In his book Jude writes that some are grumblers and complainers, rebellious sinners determined to be lost. Others will be saved, *looking for the mercy of our Lord Jesus Christ unto eternal life.* And then this: *And on some have compassion, making a distinction.* (Jude vs. 21-22)

Does God sometimes distinguish between those of us fortunate to have been born in the cradle of the faith, and others who have lived a hard but sincere life far removed from the beacons of Christian hope? Let's leave that with Him.

There is one more gentle ray of Christ's redeeming love in the Old Testament book of Zechariah. In the 13th chapter we find a prophetic description of the end times when sin and sorrow are banished. We read: *And someone will say to him, "What are these wounds in your hands?" Then he will answer, "Those with which I was wounded in the house of my friends."* (Zechariah 13:6)

Isn't that a priceless picture of what may happen in God's eternal kingdom? All of the preachers like us will stand to the side as an honest man or woman will take the nail-scarred hands of Jesus and cry out: "What happened? We don't know the story. Tell us please, how Your hands came to carry these dreadful scars."

Two questions may still be lurking in the background as you consider these issues. First of all, if God will lovingly draw many into His fold whose names don't appear on our Christian church membership books, then why should the Christian church go and passionately do missionary work? Why reach out to save people in evangelism if God can simply "extrapolate" them into heaven? It is expensive, difficult, tiring, often discouraging work to go to a foreign land, set up that tent, and preach the gospel to a foreign culture. Why do it?

First of all, we do it because we're commanded to. "Go to every nation," Jesus told His followers, and that Gospel Commission has never been rescinded. But here's a bit more: we reach out to share Jesus, not to give people their first chance, or their only chance, but their *best* chance! The best possibility of a man or woman being saved in God's kingdom is to plainly hear the story of love in the gospels . . . because it breaks and melts the heart.

True, there is a revelation of God in nature. The Spirit of God whispers to mankind through the sunrises and the sunsets, the grandeur of tall mountains and vast oceans. Many will be drawn to serve God through them. But we still want to give people the very best opportunity, because when you look at nature, it sends out mixed messages. The ocean that provides the fisherman with his meals can also reach out and snatch away his family in a tidal wave. There is a beautiful rose, but the same rose has thorns on its stem. There is the sun that warms us, but that sun can also scorch the plants and give us a sunburn. The wind provides a gentle breeze yet also brings the hurricanes that destroy homes and lives.

So in this universe, there is good and there is evil—clear heavenly signals and muddled ones. But when we look at Scripture and discover the reason for the controversy between good and evil, we find Jesus plunging Himself into the chasm of lostness on our behalf, sacrificing Himself as our Savior. So the reason we do evangelism is to give people the very best opportunity possible to know Jesus, so they can have the greatest possibility of being saved.

There is a second issue that troubles sincere Christians. Isn't it arrogant to insist that the Christian faith is "right" and the other ones "wrong?" Who are we to make such a claim? Doesn't that just divide the human race? Isn't it mostly terrorists and cultists who claim to have discovered the one true path, and that all others are lost? Wasn't it this mindset of "only us" that caused airplanes to fly into New York's twin towers?

We have both encountered this in our evangelistic travels to share the Christian message. Religious officials in the former Soviet Union have pointedly said to our It Is Written teams as we applied for visas: "Leave us be. We have our faith system already. Your arrival here will only confuse our people. You imply that you have a superior message and a better faith; what gives you the right?"

You know, if we were speaking about our own opinions, or about a theology based on our own merits or wisdom, these would be telling indictments.

But here is the response that Bishop Lesslie Newbigin once shared at a Bible conference: "If, in fact, it is true that almighty God, creator and sustainer of all that exists in heaven and on earth, has—at a known time and place in human history—so humbled Himself as to become part of our sinful humanity, and to suffer and die a shameful death to take away our sin, and to rise from the dead as the first-fruit of a new creation, if this is a fact, then to affirm it is not arrogance. *To remain quiet about it is treason to our fellow human beings.*" (From *International Review of Mission,* July 1988, pp. 325-331, quoted in *The Contemporary Christian,* p. 305)

Isn't that powerful? How could we discover a lifeboat that can save us from the sinking *Titanic,* get a coveted seat on that craft, notice that there is plenty of space for others, and then sit in mute silence as the cries of the drowning slowly fade away? No!

Any Christian who discovers the saving power of Jesus will have a burning desire to say to others: "I am no better than you. My own thoughts and ideas are frail and faulty just as yours are. But I have found the Solution to all my fears. His name is Jesus."

"If the gospel is true," writes Stanley Samartha, "[making exclusive claims] is the very best and highest way to express neighbor-love. We cannot claim to love our neighbors if we leave them in ignorance of Christ." (*The Myth of Christian Uniqueness*, pp. 79, 80)

One more question does surface, though, as we consider the Gospel Commission and the efficacy of God's saving grace. Wouldn't a loving God finally find a way, *some* way, to bring all His children home? Why is it that the Bible teaches about the saved and also the lost, and describe a broad, smooth road that takes rebels to destruction?

Look at it this way; if God overpowered human choice and took, say, all of Los Angeles to heaven, then heaven would not be heaven. It would be Los Angeles! And not the peaceful "City of Angels" pictured in the Bible! People would be beating each other up still. Gang members would be roaming the dark streets, exacting revenge on their rivals. They would be looking for crack in the back alleys. People would be hooking up with someone else's wife.

No, if God brought all of humanity to heaven, with carnal natures intact and the carnal hearts that we have, it would simply perpetuate the sin problem for eternity. Barring a mass experiment with cosmic surgery to do those "spiritual lobotomies," the human race would continue in its dysfunctional wickedness forever. And even if God believed that cosmic surgery was the solution, He would have done that six thousand years ago. Why did He make human beings with the capacity to choose if He is going to reverse that capacity at the end of time and install a new digitized mindset that is incapable of sinning?

Instead, God gives our world this free invitation: "Come! All who will—come!" But then we have to respond to the claims of His love. We have to say yes to His graciousness. We have to allow the living Christ to not only forgive our sins but also cleanse us from the habit patterns of sinning. And there will always be those who say a determined "no" to that invitation. They haven't made the choice to follow the way of love; they've chosen selfishness instead. And to choose self and the worship of self is to go down the road of rebellion to ultimate self-destruction.

The bottom line—and as our Creator, God knows this better than we do—is that somebody devoted to selfishness could never be happy in a place like heaven. It would be endless hell for them, absolute misery.

Perhaps you have heard the little parable about the people who went to their ultimate destination . . . and on both sides of the chasm, they bore the same affliction. All were plagued with these stiff, unbending arms. Apparently elbows had been banished in God's kingdom and Lucifer's alike. In hell, people sat around this table loaded with abundant delicacies; they glowered and grumbled about the fact that they couldn't eat. Nobody could get a fork or spoon up to their mouths. Resentment was rampant.

But up in heaven, with the same vast expanse of delightful morsels, the saved were unselfishly *feeding each other* and enjoying the joys of the Paradise Buffet–because the foundation of the Christian gospel is unselfishness, giving, serving, putting others first.

On the cross, Jesus sacrificed Himself so that we could have eternal life. And it's when we sacrifice ourselves to Him, that we find life. In Matthew 16:24-25 Jesus said, *If anyone desires to come after Me, let him deny himself, and take up his cross and follow Me. For whoever desires to save his life will lose it, and whoever loses his life for My sake will find it.* When we do this, we also find a desire to bring others to the same knowledge of Him. Salvation is coming to Jesus, allowing Him to forgive our sins, allowing Him to change our life, and then living a self-sacrificing, kind, compassionate life in a world of selfishness.

Friend, this is what God offers us. Do you sense why the stakes are so much higher than when we simply miss a problem on an algebra test? There's no emotional baggage attached to our value judgment that two plus two is four, and not seventeen. There are no moral implications to that. What we do with the multiplication tables doesn't require someone to change the way they live or surrender the shreds of authority and autonomy they've always clung to. In a world where the concept of moral relativity has shackled our ability to call some things right and other things wrong, it's become unpopular to suggest that some spiritual belief systems are, well, wrong. And yet simple reason tells us that everybody can't be right. Every world religion can't be right. But when Jesus says, *"I am the way, the truth, and the life. No one comes to the Father except through Me,"* (John 14:6) that demands a response from the human heart.

As God in human flesh, Jesus positioned Himself as the only key to heaven. Without the divine link He provides between God and man, there is no eternity for the human race. Tragically, most people's reluctance to accept Jesus really comes from a reluctance to take an honest look at their own lives.

Many of today's world philosophies don't demand the kind of radical change of heart spoken of in the Bible. And so many people simply take the path of least resistance, and turn to alternative religions. But is it possible that the broad path really does lead to destruction? Is it also possible that many people avoid dealing with Jesus because of a profound misunderstanding of how *He* intends to deal with them?

Centuries of religious rhetoric has given some people the idea that God delights in destroying sinners. But the truth is that He delights in destroying sin while *saving* the sinner! In the end only those who choose to cling to sin will be destroyed with it.

Today, as Jesus speaks to your heart, He's not relishing how much He would like to destroy you; He's signaling you, inviting you, wooing you to come to Him and accept His forgiveness. He doesn't want to take your freedom; He wants to restore it. He doesn't want to rob you of the delights of life; He longs to fill your life with every abundant and good thing. *"Come to Me, all you who labor and are heavy laden, and I will give you rest,"* He promises. *"Take My yoke upon you and learn from Me, for I am gentle and lowly in heart, and you will find rest for your souls. For My yoke is easy and My burden is light."* (Matthew 11:28-30)

Do you long for rest? Do you crave that elusive peace of mind? Then come, says Jesus. And friend, we promise, you'll be delighted with what you find.

Perhaps you're convinced, as we've looked at these encouraging Bible passages, that Jesus *is* the only way to salvation. You have begun to sense His incredible love for us, how much He values us, His desire to give us forgiveness and eternal life and all good things. Then—*how* do you accept Him?

There's good news for you just now. To come to Jesus is as simple as A - B - C. Really! First of all, ACCEPT that you have disobeyed Him, ACCEPT that you (along with all of us) have fallen from His grace, ACCEPT that you cannot save yourself.

Then BELIEVE that Jesus Christ, on the cross of Calvary, died the death that you deserve in order to give you the eternal life you don't deserve.

Lastly, CONFESS your sin to Him, repent and request forgiveness. Then decide you will serve Him forever.

He invites you to come! Jesus' wonderful promises are all real, and so are His invitations! He invites you to come just as you are, and be saved by His marvelous, infinite mercy, grace, and love. Why not do it right now as we pray this prayer together?

PRAYER

Dear Father in heaven, today we accept that we are all sinners. We see that it's impossible for us to save ourselves, but we believe that Your only Son, Jesus, is a mighty Savior. We believe that He did what we could never do for ourselves, and that He gave His life on a cross called Calvary in order to redeem us from sin. We tearfully and sorrowfully confess our sins, and we choose now to serve You forever, believing that RIGHT NOW You're removing the guilt and forgiving us. RIGHT NOW Your mercy and grace are flowing to us from Your own heart of love.

Father, thank You for revealing to us that Your Son, Jesus, is the exclusive way to our eternal home, but that in Your immense love, You've offered Him as an inclusive gift which takes in the entire human race. We want to be Your loyal and loving children forever. RIGHT NOW, we dedicate our lives to you, and through the power of your Holy Spirit we ask that you will help us live a life that honors you. In Jesus' saving name, Amen.

Free Bible Guides

A dynamic way to become better acquainted with your Bible.

The DISCOVER BIBLE GUIDES are designed for busy people like you. They will help bring your Bible to life and you can study at home at your own pace. No cost or obligation. The DISCOVER BIBLE GUIDES are available online or you can mail the coupon below. Or call now and begin a new adventure with your Bible.

IT IS WRITTEN

CALL TODAY
1-800-253-3000

OR LOG ONTO:
www.itiswritten.com

WE GO *by the* BOOK!

IT IS WRITTEN TELEVISION

Some things may change but our message never will.

It is written, "Man shall not live by bread alone, but by every word that proceeds from the mouth of God." *

This was the Bible text which years ago formed the foundation of this television ministry. Today we continue to share God's Word on our telecast around the globe in ten languages.

Discover a wealth of spiritual resources, Bible study guides, streaming video and a current station log at:

www.itiswritten.com

*Matthew 4:4